I LEARN FROM CHILDREN

I LEARN
—— *from* ——
CHILDREN

Caroline Pratt

Founder of The City and Country School

PERENNIAL LIBRARY

Harper & Row, Publishers, New York
Grand Rapids, Philadelphia, St. Louis, San Francisco
London, Singapore, Sydney, Tokyo, Toronto

This book was originally published in hardcover by Simon & Schuster in 1948.

I Learn From Children. Copyright © 1948, 1970 by John G. Holzwarth. All rights reserved. Printed in the United States of America. No part of this book may be used or reproduced in any manner whatsoever without written permission except in the case of brief quotations embodied in critical articles and reviews. For information address Harper & Row, Publishers, Inc., 10 East 53rd Street, New York, N.Y. 10022.

First PERENNIAL LIBRARY edition published 1990.

Library of Congress Cataloging-in-Publication Data
Pratt, Caroline
    I learn from children / Caroline Pratt. — 1st Perennial Library ed.
        p.   cm.
    Reprint. Originally published: New York : Simon and Schuster, 1948.
    ISBN 0-06-097273-4
    1. City and Country School (New York, N.Y.)—History. 2. Pratt, Caroline. 3. Women educators—Greenwich Village (New York, N.Y.)—Biography. 4. Education—Experimental methods. I. Title.
LD7501.N4945P73   1990
372.9747′1—dc20   89-45704

90 91 92 93 94 MPC 10 9 8 7 6 5 4 3 2 1

To

Helen Marot

whose spirit still lives

ACKNOWLEDGMENTS

I wish to thank Leila V. Stott for assembling material for the book, and Ruth Goode for preparing the manuscript for publication. Also I thank Max Sellers for his work and those teachers from whose records I quoted.

CONTENTS

NEW INTRODUCTION

We are excited and proud to participate in the republication of Caroline Pratt's discoveries about how children learn. This will be of great benefit to those who are involved in the current revolution in educational theory. I LEARN FROM CHILDREN can take its place beside such books as John Holt's HOW CHILDREN FAIL and HOW CHILDREN LEARN, Kornei Chukovsky's FROM TWO TO FIVE, and other works by people who really know how to observe children as they go about their most essential task of trying to make sense of the world around them.

I believe this book can contribute to the thinking of the growing multitude who want "educational relevance" for today's children. Caroline Pratt's deep understanding of children and the learning process will once again inspire those struggling to discover how the young can be given environments and opportunities that will engage their eager curiosity, their sense of joy in discovery, their deep desire to do, to make, to explore and to master.

The increasing specialization of education so that we learn more and more about less and less has had a narrowing effect on our thought. True learning based on experience should lead to knowledge, thought, wisdom, and a philosophy by which we can guide our lives. Alfred North Whitehead, the great mathematician, teacher and philosopher, wrote a marvelous book called THE AIMS OF EDUCATION in which he said: "First hand knowledge is the ultimate basis of intellectual life. To a large extent book learning conveys second hand information and as such can *never* rise to the importance of immediate practice." Ponder this as you read and consider today's educational practices. I remember reading this book and the Whitehead book at the same time—an amazing experience—and I urge you to do the same!

It is our ardent hope that the republication of this book will again inspire some of the people seeking educational truths to go forth and start new adventures in learning for children. Here you will find the story of a teacher and her school. It is a wonderful tale for today since neither she nor her staff had much use for the establishment of *their* day! Some of her most gifted teachers were entirely self-educated.

Today, many young people are crying out for an education that will meet their needs. They are seeking an experience that will build courage, imagination, story of a teacher and her school. It is a wonderful tale for today since neither she nor her staff had much use for the establishment of *their* day! Some of her most gifted teachers were entirely self-educated.

Today, many young people are crying out for an education that will meet their needs. They are seeking an experience that will build courage, imagination, self-reliance, independence and responsibility (not to mention joy and excitement), rather than boredom, despair, and self-indulgence. I believe that the discoveries of the era just passed can be used to great advantage in achieving the aims of the young people of today.

Caroline Pratt's school was staffed with people from many walks of life, all eagerly sharing the excitement of discovery themselves. This was true because she believed that real learning depends upon first-hand discovery. Otherwise "too much verbal information" gets in the child's way. The school they created grew and throve, and gradually a curriculum evolved which was based on close observation of and work with children. The activities they offered either met the constant needs of children or they were discarded.

Today there is an outcry for smaller schools. Indeed this is essential if children are to learn to know themselves and each other and to feel part of their community. However, mere size is not enough. The experiences children have and the grownups with whom they work make the important difference between success and failure.

Today's children often have a rough bewildering time. Never before has the commercial world bombarded them (and of course their parents) with so much noise, instant entertainment, distraction, confusion, violence and disparate bits of information. With ears and eyes besieged by the sounds and sights of our frenetic mass media they find it difficult to pursue their own discoveries. How can children make sense of a world which appears to be overwhelming to so many grownups? That question brings us right back to the importance of the school, particularly with reference to the fact the children must have an opportunity to fulfill responsibilities.

When given a chance, children grow wonderfully self-reliant and are proud of their increasing skills and accomplishments. They develop self-respect, understanding of others and their own standards of excellence. Well-meaning adults who put more values on young children's products (art, poetry, music, plays) than on the value gained by *making* them, and rush to frame their pictures and publish their writing, often confuse the children. The young learn best by continuous experimentation; not from excessive display of the results of their handiwork.

Opportunity for children to assume responsibility is an especially interesting aspect of the curriculum in the light of today's problems. The pride the eight year olds take in the postal services they run, the nines in their store, and the elevens in the work of their print shop cannot be over-emphasized. The entire social studies and history program takes off from these jobs, and often music, science, dramatics and art are woven in as well.

The job of the twelve year olds has been added since this book was first written and I'd like to mention it briefly, especially since the children consider it the best of all. They help to look after the four year olds, make books, sing songs, make up plays and sometimes design and construct toys for them. They become fast friends and the older ones often return to see how "their fours" are growing up. Their observations are usually astute and always concerned.

If the reprinting of I LEARN FROM CHILDREN does no more than inspire the establishment of one more good place in which children can grow and learn, it will have been entirely worthwhile. If it also helps some people to sort out their confusions about educational theories and perhaps gives them a few touchstones for evaluating them it will also have been worthwhile.

Can the schools of the future find ways in which to help children understand and cope with *their* world? Can they "fit the school to the child, not the child to the school"? Will they be able to develop in children the kind of thinking and working attitude that will enable them to take over their own growth and make a better world for living? Thoughtful students everywhere are asking for this kind of education. Perhaps it is their turn to evolve schools for young children as well as for themselves.

Over thirty years of close association with children has given me great faith in their potential. I believe they can and will find solutions to our current confusions.

JEAN W. MURRAY, Principal
City and Country School

AUTHOR'S FOREWORD

How UTTERLY the life of a child in this country has changed during my lifetime I would scarcely believe if I had not seen it happen. Three-quarters of a century have spanned the change: my father was a Civil War veteran; I remember the day we all went down to the store to see my mother make our first call on a telephone; I remember watching the explosive progress of the first automobile down our village street.

Put it this way, as the statistics put it: before 1867, the year I was born, only one out of every six people lived in cities of more than 8,000 inhabitants, and there were only 141 such cities; by 1900, one out of three people lived in such a city, and the number of those cities was 547. (I quote from Leo Huberman's *America, Incorporated*.) Nearly half a century has passed since 1900, and the transition from rural and village life to a big-city industrial civilization is a half-century farther along.

I have seen the world of the child grow smaller and smaller. From the wide wonderful place of my childhood, it has become a narrow cell, walled about with the mysteries of complex machinery and the hazards of a motor-driven urban setting.

When I grew up in Fayetteville, New York, school was not very important to children who could roam the real world freely for their learning. We did not merely stand by while the work of our simpler world was done; I drove the wagon in haying time, sitting on top of the swaying load, all the way to the barn. At ten, my great-aunt used to say, I could turn a team of horses and a wagon in less space than a grown man needed to do it.

No one had to tell us where milk came from, or how butter was made. We helped to harvest wheat, saw it ground into flour in the mill on our own stream; I baked bread for the family at thirteen. There was a paper mill, too, on our stream; we could learn the secrets of half a dozen other industries merely by walking through the open door of a neighbor's shop.

No wonder school was a relatively unimportant place—a place where we learned only the mechanical tools, the three R's, and a smattering about things far away and long ago. Our really important learning, the learning how to live in the world into which we were born and how to participate in its work, was right at hand, outside the schoolhouse walls.

This is the change I have seen, from a world in which children could learn as they grew in it, to a world so far beyond the grasp of children, that only the school can present it to them in terms which they can understand, can prepare them with knowledge of it so that they can take their places in it with confidence when the time comes.

This is why, between my eightieth and my eighty-first birthday, I have sat down to tell the story of my own adventure in the teaching of children, an adventure which has absorbed me during an entire lifetime.

I began the adventure innocently enough when at sixteen I became the teacher of a one-room school not far from Fayetteville. It was my great-uncle Homer's idea, possibly born of the neighbors' endorsement, "Carrie was always good with children." I next taught first grade in our village school, and when the children and I were thoroughly weary of the three R's, I varied the program by teaching the little boys to tip their hats to a woman.

Nevertheless a neighbor was kind enough to think I had possibilities as a teacher, and to speak to the Dean of Teachers College in New York. Out of this came an offer of a scholarship, which I eagerly accepted.

Two years later I was teaching young women to saw to a line, in the Manual Training shop of the Philadelphia Normal School. It was here, truthfully, that my education really began. Restless as I was under the curriculum imposed upon me by the traditional system of the day, I sought in every direction for guidance toward new ways of teaching. I took courses at the University of Pennsylvania, and was fortunate enough to encounter the iconoclast Charles Henderson there. I subscribed for courses from the University of Chicago. My seven years of teaching in Philadelphia became a period of intensive self-education.

Since the day in 1901 when I resigned from the Normal School and went to New York to seek a way of carrying out my own ideas in teaching, my education has been given me at the hands of children themselves. What I know of children I have learned from them. There have been moments when I have felt like Columbus discovering a new continent, and, conversely, many times when the uncharted world of childhood has presented no clear path by which a mere adult could find her way in it.

The story of this exploration into the world of children and their ways of growing and learning is what I have set down here. If it helps some children by making their ways of learning a little clearer to some parents and some teachers, I shall be well content.

C. P.

I LEARN FROM CHILDREN

CHAPTER ONE
WHAT IS A SCHOOL?

OFTEN DURING my three decades in the City and Country School I have thought we should have a doctor on hand at all times. Not for the children (we took care of that) but for innocent visitors to our classrooms. Sometimes, emerging from a morning of observation, they have seemed visibly to be suffering from shock!

This was not likely to be true of mothers—a mother more often came away from her first visit with a look of bewildered pleasure. She had watched a group of happy children without always knowing what they were happy about, but for the moment it was enough that they were happy.

Occasionally a father looked jolted, worried; how, in that turmoil, would his son ever get ready for Harvard?

But the sharpest reaction could be counted on to come from the good teacher whose entire life had been spent in a traditional classroom.

"Do you call this a school?" She would ask the question in terms more or less politely veiled depending on how far her principles had been outraged. And I could sympathize with her, having served my time in the kind of classroom where each child sits on a bench nailed to the floor, at a desk as firmly fixed in its place, incommunicado as far as all the other children are concerned—and the teacher at the front of the room sternly bound to maintain the discipline without which, it is assumed, the work will not get done.

I have put such a teacher among, say, our sixth-graders, the Elevens, to share a part of their full and busy day. By contrast to the nailed-down dependability of her own classroom, here nothing was fixed, nothing stayed put, not even the furniture; above all, not the children!

Some would be in the print room, turning out a job. There they were anchored at least to the presses; yet through the wide doorway there would be a constant movement of active young bodies round and round among type cases and stock shelves, with a chatter of voices as continuous as the hum and clatter of the presses. Orders, comments, criticisms, a shouted question to the teacher from the foreman-of-the-week: "We finished the Sevens' reading work—shall we start on the library card order or the Parents' Association letterheads?"

Within the classroom itself there would be no stillness, either visual or auditory. Treble howls of disagreement might be rising from the corner where the editorial committee of the Elevens' magazine, soon going to press, debated the literary merits of a nine-year-old's story—or a Thirteen's, the more sharply criticized because of the author's advanced age. A pig-tailed Eight bounded into the room, her small face solemnly on duty bent, a canvas mail pouch hanging from her shoulders; postman from the Eights' post-office, she carried a Special Delivery letter, an invitation to the Elevens from the Tens to attend a performance of their play in the Gym the next morning. Two Elevens returned, laden with packages of paper, pencils, notebooks, jars of bright paints, supplies bought for the group at the school store run by the Nines. A tall Twelve, splotches of mimeographing ink competing with the freckles on his nose, carried in a stack of copies of *The Yardbird*, weekly newspaper published by his group, to be sold later at 1¢ apiece. (The price, I understand, has recently risen to 3¢—another case of rising costs of production.)

Half a dozen Elevens might now bang in from work in the science room, the clay room, the shop, and you could tell which, for the marks of their labors would be plain on their worn and stained dungarees. With the new arrivals there would be a shifting of tables and chairs, a foraging in lockers to get out an arithmetic book which needed correcting, a linoleum cut to be finished, a topic—Astronomy in the Middle Ages—to be written up in a notebook. The teacher might be asked, "How much time before Yard?" but rarely, "What shall we do now?" Each child apparently knew what unfinished work he had on hand and promptly applied himself to it. From the class treasurer of the week, pushing a lock of brown hair behind an ear while she worked on her accounts, there might come a piteous wail—"We'll have to stop losing pencils! If we have to buy pencils again this week we can't afford the trip to Chinatown!"

And swirling around the visitor's head, beating against her unaccustomed ears, there was *noise*, until the walls of the room must bulge with it. Of twenty souls in the room, only one was quiet—the teacher.

Of course the visitor was right in her complaint: this did not look or sound like any schoolroom. But it was very much like something else. It was like a segment of grown-up activity, an office, a small factory, or perhaps office and factory combined. Nor did these children look like school children, starched and clean-faced, the boys in white shirts, the girls in crisp frocks. These children wore work-clothes, dungarees or overalls, boys and girls alike (occasionally a dress, the exercise of individual prerogative), and they and their work-clothes bore the evidences of their work. "Do they have to get so dirty?" mothers have been asking for thirty years. But was there ever a printer without ink on his trousers and his cheek, a cook without flour on her elbows and aprons?

This classroom was a place where work was done. The workers could not be fastened down; they had to come and go about their various jobs, fetch supplies, seek advice, examine, compare, discuss. The work got done, not in proportion to the silence in the room, but in proportion to the responsibility of each worker to his job and to the group. Some were more able, more responsible workers than others—as among adults. And, as among adults, there was a supervisor (not a boss, however) directing, counseling, channeling the abundant energies of these young workers, keeping the balance among personalities, keeping the schedule of the day's program and its constantly varying tasks, checking the accomplishment of both group and individual.

No wonder the visitor was confounded. The movement bewildered her; the noise came between her and the work. But she was the only one in the room who was bewildered.

She could not see the pattern, so unlike the traditional one with which she was familiar, so much more complex. Yet it was an obvious and familiar pattern, seen everywhere except in the traditional schoolroom. It was the traditional pattern, rather than this one, which was strange and unfamiliar. This one was the normal pattern of human activity, adult or child. Because these were children, the noise was louder, the movement more explosive. And because these were children, the task of the teacher and her student-teacher assistant was so much more than merely that of a shop foreman or a supervisor in an adult project that here, in truth, the analogy breaks down. This teacher had a task so subtle, so exacting, that a traditionally trained teacher could scarcely hope to comprehend it at a glance.

And if she asked us, as in one way or another she always did, is this a school—we could ask in our turn, *what is a school?*

To answer that a school is a place of learning is no answer at all, but only another way of stating the question. A place of learning what? A place of learning, *how?*

I was seventeen when I taught my first class—a one-room school in the country—and I had had none of the benefits of normal school, teacher training, nor even, possibly, had ever heard the word *pedagogy*. What I did have was a deep conviction, unspoken, indeed unconscious until much later, that a desire to learn was as natural and inevitable in children as the desire to walk in babies.

How could anyone doubt that it was? Once beyond the eating-sleeping stage, every day, every hour of a young child's waking life is devoted to adventure, exploration, discovery of the world around him. His fiercest struggles are to learn—to turn over, to sit up, to walk, to climb; later, to grasp a toy, to shake a rattle, to roll and recapture a ball; still later, to investigate the working of light switches, telephones, clocks. ("Why must he be so *destructive?*" protests the dismayed mother, but our forefathers had to see their houses burned down before they knew how fire worked.) His greatest frustrations, aside from his own limitations, are the restrictions placed upon him by the adult world in his effort to touch, to feel, to see and smell and taste. And his method of learning? The first and best one, the one used by Neanderthal man and by the atomic scientist—trial and error.

No one who has watched a baby return to his lessons day after day—and persist in them despite bumps and bruises—can doubt the drive of the young human being to learn. And indeed if man did not have this compulsion to explore, to understand, and to conquer or at least come to terms with the world in which he lives, including his own person, he must surely have disappeared from the earth ages ago, along with the millions of other forms of life which have vanished, even the mighty dinosaur.

But something happens, alas, to this great driving force. All but a very few men and women in the world, a few unique beings touched with some kind of genius, have lost the urge to learn.

They lost it, in fact, long before they were grown. They lost it while they were still little children, while they were still spending their days in the place of learning, the school—perhaps that was where they lost it!

A visitor from out of town—not an educator, merely a perceptive and sensitive mother—told me something once which I have never forgotten. She had spent an hour or two in the school, and sat down with me afterward to talk about her own boys, who were pupils at a fine traditional private school.

"When they were six they were so busy, so active, so alive!" she said. "They had so many interests, wanted to do so many things—and did them! Now they are eleven and nine, and it's all gone. They have no interest, no curiosity, no initiative or imagination or individuality. They might have been turned out in a factory." I can remember that there were tears in her eyes.

Maybe because circumstances had made me a teacher, and maybe because I was a teacher before I learned the accepted ways to teach—whatever the reason, I was in my twenties when I began to look for the child's lost desire to learn. It seemed to me that if we could keep this desire alive through childhood and into adult life, we would release a force more precious and powerful for good than any physical force the scientists ever discovered for mankind's use.

At least, I reasoned, it would make the years of learning, the school years, meaningful. The child would learn in such a way that his knowledge would actually go with him from the schoolroom into the world; his knowledge would become part of him, as the knowledge the infant gains by his own trial and error method becomes part of him.

I had seen fifteen-year-old boys who had been faithfully taught their three R's in the public school struck dumb and helpless when they needed to divide a fifteen-inch board into two halves in the shop. It was only one evidence—but how revealing—of what I had seen again and again, that our teaching had failed to teach, that it had only crammed knowledge like excelsior into unreceptive little heads, knowledge that was unused because it was unusable as we had given it, unrelated, undigested. Most dreadful of all, unwanted.

I once asked a cooking teacher why she did not let the children experiment with the flour and yeast, to see whether they could make bread. She said in a shocked voice, "But that would be so wasteful!"

She was no more shocked by my question than I by her answer. That materials used in education should be considered wasted! Ours must be a strange educational system, I thought. And, of course, the more I studied it, the more convinced I became that it was very strange indeed. It was saving of materials, ah yes—but how wasteful of children!

Once in our school I watched a little girl take sheets of good drawing paper, one by one, from a pile—I counted up to fifty. She made a little mark on each one with a crayon, and threw it away. Fifty sheets of paper wasted, and nobody said, "Don't!" On the contrary, when she stopped and looked fearfully at the teacher, she got a smile and an encouraging,

"Try another one." That little girl was in school for the first time, and terrified. She could not speak at all, could not look at the teacher without shriveling. Those fifty sheets of paper were a beginning for her; she drew, then played with blocks, then answered the child who played beside her on the floor, and in a few weeks she had begun to find her way through the jungle of her own terrors and was learning to be a happy, busy little school girl.

Yes, no doubt we are wasteful of paper and paints and clay and wood and a few pounds of flour and a few cents' worth of yeast. But we try not to waste the child, or his energies, or his time. I have seen time wasted in the traditional classroom, where out of forty children one is reciting, while thirty-nine sit with empty hands, empty faces—and empty heads. I have seen a little boy with his chin in his hand and his eyes on the door, doing nothing, thinking nothing, only waiting with dreadful resignation for the moment when the bell would ring and the door would open, and he could get out of school.

But the child, unhampered, does not waste time. Not a minute of it. He is driven constantly by that little fire burning inside him, to do, to see, to learn. You will not find a child anywhere who will sit still and idle unless he is sick—or in a traditional classroom.

How this unnatural treatment of children came about was not my concern. I would not, even if I could, go into the history of education, a course in which I was an unhappy failure at Teachers College so many years ago. My own education was given me, not in teacher-training courses, not by professors of pedagogy, but by children themselves.

A child playing on his nursery floor, constructing an entire railroad system out of blocks and odd boxes he had salvaged from the wastepaper basket, taught me that the play impulse in children is really a work impulse. Childhood's work is learning, and it is in his play—before he ever gets into the hands of teachers in organized education—that the child works at his job. No child ever lavished on a history book the energy he poured into a game of cowboys and Indians. But cowboys and Indians are a part of the history of our country which he must learn. What is wrong with learning history by playing it?

Surely the school was at fault, not the child. Was it unreasonable to try to fit the school to the child, rather than—as we were doing with indifferent success—fitting the child to the school?

I sometimes thought, in my rebellious twenties, that the educators had never seen a child. It is one thing to have a child handed you, as the traditional teacher is handed her young charges, at the age of five or six—and then to proceed with him according to the curriculum. But that is not to *see* a child, any more than looking at a lion in a zoo is to see a lion.

To see a child means seeing him in terms of his own horizons, and almost from the day he is born. You see then how the circle of his interest widens outward, like the circles made by a stone thrown into a pond. First he is concerned with his own person—his hands and feet, the motion of his body. Then his mother's face, his crib, his nursery floor, the house in which he lives and the people in it, the milkman and the grocer's boy who deliver his food, the street and the park in which he plays.

Children "play house," and how ill we understand the word "play." They are working in deadly earnest at the job of preparing to be adults, with the most serious of adult responsibilities, that of parenthood. A little girl pinned into a big apron stirs the batter for a cake—a favorite magazine advertisement in full color, favorite because it is quaint. Instead of cooing over her quaintness, we should treat her with respect. She is learning to be a mother in her own kitchen some day, learning to cook with loving care for the health and enjoyment of her own family.

Again and again in my life of learning from children I have remembered my own childhood, and that eager desire to help grown-ups in grown-up work—only to be given the lowliest and least interesting chores to do. How happily I would have washed the pots and pans, if I had had a hand in the cooking that was done in them! But that would have been wasteful; I might have spilled or spoiled good food. Perhaps it would be wasteful in the home when a limited budget must actually feed the family (although even of this I am not convinced). But a school is a place of learning; what economy have we served if we have wasted the urge to learn?

Children have their own meaning for the word *play*. To them it does not, as it does to adults, carry the ideas of idleness, purposelessness, relaxation from work. When we began our school we had named it a "play school," as a telegraphic way of saying that in our way of teaching, the children learned by playing. It was the children who made us, early in the school's history, delete the word from the school's name. To them it was not a "play school" but a school, and they were working hard at their schooling.

How hard they work, only we who have watched them really know. They do not waste one precious moment. They are going about their jobs all the time. No father in his office or mother in her home works at such a pace. For a long time I was principally afraid that they would exhaust themselves in this strenuous new kind of school.

Every step of the way, I was learning too. I had set myself the task of learning where, in our teaching of children, we were letting the precious desire to learn dribble wastefully away. I was going to find the leak in the dike and put my finger in it. Often it seemed to me that there were too many leaks, that the ponderous system we had erected for bringing children up both in school and in the home resembled more a sieve than a dike. I found myself going back toward the beginning, earlier and earlier in the child's life.

I followed the urge to learn through some of its many aspects. I saw it as the urge to play: at the moment that we scorned this impulse and set it aside, and treated it as something apart from serious work, at that moment we were beginning to waste the child.

I saw the urge to see, touch, experience everything at

first hand. At the moment that we interpose second-hand knowledge—from the teacher instead of from the world itself, from books rather than from life—again we have begun to waste the child. True, there comes a time in a child's learning about his constantly expanding world when he can no longer go out and see for himself. For the far-away and long-ago he must turn to books and museums. But the moment when he must begin to do his learning from second-hand sources is a critical one. If we thrust him toward it too soon, before he has learned to gather his facts and relate them for himself, to ask his own questions and find his own answers, then we have opened another breach through which the desire to learn can be lost.

And I saw, too, the urge to learn with a purpose, purpose that is immediate, practical, and within the scope of a child to understand. It is as much good to a child to know his three R's by rote, to have been poured full of knowledge of skills without the ability to use them, as it is to a man to know the principles of swimming and not be able to save himself from drowning.

It has taken me a lifetime of learning from children to begin to know these things: how to stop the waste, how to channel the precious forces of children.

CHAPTER TWO

FIRST EXPERIMENTS

I THINK the first time I questioned seriously our accepted method of teaching children was one day in our Kindergarten course at Teachers College, when our instructor, a little plump woman, bounded suddenly to her feet and began to circle about the room, fluttering her arms.

"Now we will all dance like butterflies!" she commanded, and we all rose up in our starched shirtwaists and long skirts

and our high-buttoned shoes, big-boned Westerners and dec-
orous New Englanders and up-State country girls like myself, and obediently fluttered after her.

There were other matters, besides the command to dance
like a butterfly, which troubled me as I went from lecture to
lecture in the old building on University Place in downtown
New York. To study at Teachers College was considered
quite an advanced thing to do, in the year 1892, and we were
a proud group of females from all over the country, bent on
taking the newest thought back with us to the classrooms of
our home towns. Because I had always been interested in
young children, the career of a Kindergartner seemed most
appealing to me. But the more I learned of the newest Kindergarten methods of the day, the more uncertain I became.

Little children, we were taught, should begin the school
day by sitting quietly in a circle. They could sing or have a
story read, but the sitting in a circle was the important thing.
This would give them an awareness of the unity of human
life. There was a good deal of this mystical fol-de-rol, and
to my practical mind it was more like learning to walk a
tight-rope than to teach any children I had ever met.

It had a practical value, as I have since come to understand,
though not one with which I could have the slightest sympathy. You taught children to dance like butterflies, when
you knew they would much rather roar like lions, because
lions are hard to discipline and butterflies aren't. All activity
in the Kindergarten must be quiet, unexciting. All of it was
designed to prepare the children for the long years of discipline ahead. Kindergarten got them ready to be bamboozled
by the first grade.

My first act of rebellion, then, was to go to the Dean
and announce that Kindergarten was not for me. Guessing
rightly that country living had given me a capable pair of
hands, he suggested Arts and Crafts. Soon I was happily hammering and sawing in the Manual Training shop.

My happiness, however, was short-lived. This was not
the last time I was to spoil my own fun by asking questions.

In the shop I had been learning to use one tool after another (someone had decided which were easier and which harder, and the tools were given us in that order), and to perform one kind of operation after another (someone had also decided the order of difficulty for these). I sawed to a line; I planed; I chiseled. I made joints, one after another, until I reached the crowning achievement, the blind dovetail. But I never made a single object! This was the way I was to teach Manual Training to children when I was a graduate teacher.

Today this perhaps sounds incredible. Think of swarms of children all over the country, busy bees in Manual Training shops—sawing, chiseling, hammering—and never making a thing! But that was traditional education. Your curriculum was a series of exercises, graded from easy to difficult. Your pupils had to master one skill after another—and all in the abstract, all carefully skirting around any practical application, all strictly in accord with the idea that education was practice, but never by the slightest taint practical!

Now it is all very well to ask an adult to devote himself to an exercise purely for the improvement of his technique. An adult—or rather, most adults—can understand that there is something gained in the end. But it took no giant imagination to realize that this could not be true of the children whom I was eventually to teach by the same method.

No, no. A box, a little table, maybe even a wobbly three-legged stool. But not just a series of joints, however skillful. A child had to make something tangible, functional; something, however simple, that he could at least see the use of; ideally, something that he could himself use. The adult purpose of *getting ready* to produce something was too long-range a prospect to enlist the whole attention of a child. An exercise in the making of a blind dovetail would never bring to life the purposeful effort which I was beginning to recognize as the essence of education.

This was the kind of thinking which would give me no peace. It buzzed with insect persistence through my head as I bent to my work in the Manual Training shop. When after two years they gave me my diploma—reluctantly, I thought —and I went to my first job, this kind of thinking stung me into acute dissatisfaction.

I went directly from Teachers College to the teaching of Manual Training in the Normal School for Girls in Philadelphia. Naturally, I used the system I had been taught—I knew no other—but I taught with the depressing conviction that I was helping to perpetuate a system which had no real educational value. My students would in turn become teachers; they would go out to spread the system further. What I was doing was as unfair to them, I felt, as it would be later to the children they would teach.

I sought for something I could do to make my work in the Normal School worth while for my students, something which would have positive value for them in their own later teaching. I decided to go to Sweden for a summer course at the Sloyd School, whose reputation—of peculiar interest to me—rested on the introduction into Manual Training of a set of "useful models."

Teachers came from many countries to take the course, and the contact with them was stimulating. I learned a goodly number of new processes in handwork. At the end of the course I had several "useful" articles to take home. But when I took stock of them, among the egg-whippers, butter paddles, salad forks and other objects which some able housewife might cherish in her kitchen, I found only one—a sugar scoop —which was useful to me. And I entertained the most serious doubts whether any of them would satisfy a child's eager desire. Essentially they were, like the series of joints leading up to a blind dovetail, graduated exercises in skill. So my journey was on the whole a disappointment; I had only a lame answer to my question.

If I could not get what I sought from others, I must work it out for myself. My first effort, after my return to Philadelphia, was to see just how valid was the assumption that one operation is fundamentally easier than another. I worked in the shop to demonstrate the proposition, the while I taught the girls of the Normal School to saw to a line—and in the end I was satisfied that the difference in learning one kind of operation as against another was actually so slight as to be negligible. They were different, but not necessarily easier or harder to perform. This was the first practical confirmation of my belief that the system of graded exercises was basically unsound. And there the case rested until I could find an opportunity for further investigation.

I did some other, perhaps more important, learning for my future work, quite outside both the Normal School and my courses at the University. My guide was a young librarian with a Quaker background and a profound concern for human values.

Helen Marot later became known for her work in the organization of the Women's Trade Union League in New York, and for her two books on labor, *American Trade Unions* and *Creative Impulse in Industry*. When I met her, she and a likeminded friend had established a small library which had become a center of liberal thought in Philadelphia. People of all shades of radicalism came there—Single Taxers, Socialists, philosophical anarchists—attracted by the unusual books and periodicals and no less by the opportunity for discussion.

I took to spending a good deal of time there myself. With my own adventures in learning ever on my mind, I saw there still another aspect of education. Listening to these people, many of them graybeards, as they argued and studied, I began to see education not as an end in itself, but as the first step in a progress which should continue during a lifetime.

Most people considered their education finished when they finished school. But it seemed to me that a school's job was quite the opposite—not to finish, but to begin education. A lifetime is not too long to spend in learning about the world. A school's function could become that of developing in children the kind of thinking and working attitudes which would enable them to take over their own future growth. Looked at in this way, education became to me a new and living thing!

During my last year in Philadelphia I worked only half time at the Normal School. The other half was spent in helping Helen Marot in an investigation of the custom tailoring trade, the results of which were later published in a United States Department of Labor bulletin.

It was for me a bitter eye-opener, that experience. The work was done in the home, with no limit to the hours the people worked, and no check on working conditions—which were also living conditions, and which from both points of view were appalling. The contrast with educational practice as I knew it was painful. Helen and I often discussed the futility of trying to reform the school system, if after leaving school human beings had to earn their living under such conditions as these. As a district nurse said of a family of Italians who lived in a basement, "Their plants die in the little clay pots, but the children live." It seemed to me that a school's greatest value must be to turn out human beings who could think effectively and work constructively, who could in time make a better world than this for living in.

The time came when I went out to seek a way to put my own ideas about learning into practice. I resigned from the Normal School and went back to New York.

I found three jobs, one in a small private school, the other two in settlement houses. In all three of them I would have a free hand in the running of Manual Training shops. There were no restrictions of curriculum to bind me, and the three jobs could run concurrently. I accepted them all.

I began by telling the children that they could make what they pleased, and that I was there to help them if they ran into trouble. I had a few simple models about the shop— a boat, some boxes, a few pieces of doll furniture—so that the children would not be embarrassed if they could think of nothing to make. My teaching consisted of advising them not to be too ambitious at first; to state clearly what they wanted to make by drawing a plan of it before they began to work. As they worked, I went about among them, corrected their use of tools when necessary, showed them easy methods of getting where they wanted to go. I had only one rule: *work or leave the shop.*

No doubt it was the absence of other rules which made this one, at first, a little difficult to enforce. Little by little, though, the one rule began to reveal its strength. Children who had come in merely to make a row either stayed to work or dropped away. A few of the settlement boys wanted both to make a row and to work. I passed by many of their impertinences entirely and made little fuss about others, and by keeping my own eye strictly on the work in hand I succeeded in holding them to it. The satisfaction of purposeful effort—and the visible results—won them over in the end, as I had always believed it would.

I remember the day Pete capitulated. Pete was one of the tough boys, an apprentice to the gangster profession, and I could expect trouble whenever he appeared in the shop. I was crossing the court on the way up to the shop when a voice yelled to me out of the shop window.

"Hurry up and get up here, Merry Sunshine!" the voice shouted. I looked up and saw Pete grinning and waving to me. In the stern tradition in which I had been trained, this would have been considered an infringement of the respect due me as a teacher, a dent in my authority over my class. But I bounded up the stairs, happy in the knowledge that Pete was now on the side of the law, at least in my little domain. From then on, with only occasional lapses, Pete was in fact a self-appointed enforcement officer of the shop's one rule.

The one-rule method worked as well in the private school as in the two settlements. Other aspects of my teaching practice worked, I was soon forced to admit, even better with these children of privileged homes. They rattled off ideas for things to make with much greater readiness; their richer opportunities to play, to travel about, generally to become familiar with the world around them, even the mere fact of having more and varied possessions, gave them a wealth of suggestions for things to reproduce in the shop. The work with them was easier—but it never seemed quite so important as with the others. There was no satisfaction in the private school which compared with the harder accomplishment of offering new opportunities to children who needed them so desperately, and who used them with such intelligence and joy.

Judged by traditional standards, the boxes, stools, and toys we produced in my three shops were no doubt rather crude. But perfect technique was not my first concern. What was important was to have the children plan their own work, think it through, carry it out as much as possible by themselves. I waited wherever I could for the question to come from the child; I stepped in only when the child was puzzled, or to show him a short cut for what he was doing the hard way. Learning came not only by doing, but by thinking and planning the doing as well. Crude as the end result might be, if the child was satisfied with what he had produced, that was all I asked. His standards would improve with his skill. In fact, it was vital that his standards should not be too high for his abilities, or he would be discouraged before he ever began.

In time the children made me proud of them. They became expert little shop workers, filled with the deepest of satisfactions. It is not easy to fool a child into thinking he has done something by himself; he knows where the skilled hand of the grown-up has intervened. But these children knew that the entire work of production—thinking, planning, executing—was all theirs, and the knowledge opened for them a fascinating world into which they walked with confidence in their own powers.

The settlement classes gave me my first contact with public-school children since I had left the village school in Fayetteville. It was a saddening revelation. These children spent almost ten months of the year at school, five days a week, five hours a day—and yet, I found, the time had been of little use to them. Their program had been aimed at mastering the three R's, the tools of learning. It was to provide them with the skills of daily activity and the entrance into the world of books. But none of these children made any use of what they had learned.

They did not read, shirked any occasion to write, and could not call upon what little arithmetic they knew to help them in their work. I had to teach the simple arithmetic we used in the shop. Often the mere mention of a fractional part was enough to block the minds of these fourteen- and fifteen-year-old boys so that it was impossible for them to think. I am not exaggerating: those boys had not learned to think even in simple arithmetical terms; they were thrown into a panic when the need arose for them to do so.

A somewhat ludicrous but none the less real problem arose in my work at the settlements: I found that the families from which these children came were so cramped for space that there was no room for the articles the children so proudly brought home from the shop. This was not funny to the child who saw the toy ice wagon, on the making of which he had spent so many earnest hours, thrown out by an irate father who tripped over it in the dark of their crowded, littered tenement flat. I saw that there were practical restrictions on what the children could make, beyond the limitations of their own skill, and I sought for objects which children would enjoy making and using, and which would not be so bulky as to cause confusion at home. It was harder to find such models than one would expect. I compromised finally on some imported wooden toys which did not satisfy altogether but had at least the virtue of compactness.

It was during this search that I had an experience which deeply affected all my subsequent thinking. With my mind full of questions about what kind of toys would best fit children's own purposes and the spatial limitations of their homes, I went one day to see a friend who had an interesting young son. He was an inventive and ingenious six-year-old, and I never missed an opportunity to look in on him in his nursery. On this occasion I found the floor covered with a miniature railroad system. He was building with blocks, toys, odd paper boxes, and any material he could find. Some of it was obviously salvaged from the wastepaper basket. As I watched him push his freight train onto a siding while a fast express roared by to stop at a station where lines of passengers and automobiles were waiting, as I listened to the unceasing accompaniment of happy noises in realistic imitation of train whistles and bells and automobile horns—it seemed to me that this child had discovered an activity more satisfying to him than anything I had ever seen offered to children.

It was a fascinating thought that came to me, pressed against the wall of that nursery so as not to get in the way of the busy miniature world he had created there. I thought that this was one little boy's way of learning about the world he lived in; he had observed for himself, had gathered his facts, and was here, before my eyes, writing the perfect child's textbook of what he had seen. Here, in a combination of map, model, and working drawing with sound track—such a combination as had never existed in any classroom, more's the pity—he was setting down his understanding of the way things worked, the relationships of facts to each other, the causes and effects, the purposes and functions. This was thinking, this was learning. This was the way a young child, if freed to do so, would go about educating himself on the subject which was of most immediate, intense interest to him—the world in which he lived.

The scene was to me a nearly perfect picture of child activity, nearly but not quite. One thing was lacking: the presence of collaborators of his own age. Rich as was his own contribution, ingenious as was his invention, even so happily endowed a child as this could benefit from the give and take of his own contemporaries, the pooling of their experiences and ideas.

I yearned to see a child world peopled with such happy children as this little boy. My thinking raced toward the conclusion that such activity—play activity—might be developed into an ideal means of teaching young children. But I had no opportunity to try it in any of my three jobs.

Finally this idea so took possession of me that I resigned from the settlements and the private school. I had a new plan. Instead of teaching, I would make toys which could be used in dramatic play of this kind, play which would reproduce the children's experience with their own environment. The toys were related in size and function, and were so designed that they could be used by the children to portray familiar activities such as barn, house, or street schemes.

I carefully kept the toys simple in construction so that they could be used as models if the children desired to make others along the same line. I named my brain-children Do-Withs—and for a time I had high hopes that I had created something that would revolutionize education.

Alas for happy innocence! I realized—most practically, as I thought—that I could not expect to introduce such an innovation into the school system single-handed, but I thought I had a way around this obstacle. If the toys could be made commercially successful, I reasoned, their use as an educational medium might follow. And I actually found a manufacturer who was willing to go into the venture.

Mr. Castleman and I worked together long enough to wish that we had never met, for the toys were a total failure. Perhaps my supposed mistrust of parents—of which friends have accused me during most of my life—dates from this time, for it is parents, after all, who buy toys, and they greeted my offering of a new kind of playthings with a colossal lack of interest. To expect them to leap upon the Do-Withs uttering cries of delighted discovery was, after all, rather unreasonable of me; I did not take them into my confidence and explain the idea behind the toys. No effort was made to promote them as a new approach to play—and if we had made the effort, I very much fear it would have made no difference in their reception.

One conference with Mr. Castleman remains in my memory, a bit brighter than most of our discussions. He came one day to tell me how much he had lost on the toys. It was not

Caroline Pratt

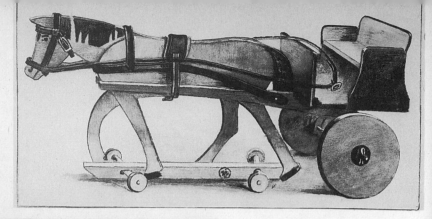

Caroline Pratt's original drawings for the "Do-With" toys for The Toy Company.

First classrooms at McDougal Alley—

and early days on
West Twelfth Street.

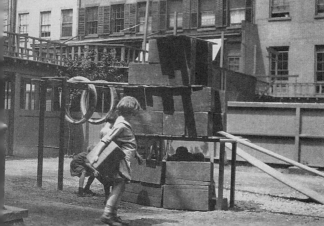

a heartening recital—until he plaintively went on to say that it was not the loss of money that hurt him most. The discipline of his factory had been ruined! The Do-Withs had made toy designers of his workers overnight, and it took him three days to get them back into routine, three days of further losses. Somehow I couldn't feel too sorry. At least the men had had a good time.

The fact that my first and only business venture lived and died without making the faintest mark on the world did not grieve me unduly. It did, however, drop me all at once into a curious lull, after so much feverish activity, a lull which had the salutary effect of making me stop to catch my breath and, most important, to take stock.

My commercial attempt taught me only a negative lesson: there is no quick and easy way to press your idea upon the world, however brightly it may glow with promise—to your eyes—of great good. I might count myself lucky to have got off merely with loss of time and of a good and honest businessman's money; greater innovators have lost far more.

But from the children in my three teaching jobs I had learned quite a good deal. I had established the value of allowing them to make what they wanted to; the method had proved successful enough to keep the shop filled with busy, eager workers.

The many failures, however, worried me. Children came, worked a while, and then dropped out. The shelves were full of abandoned pieces. Actually the shop relied upon a group of picked children who had the ability to carry an idea through. Yet they too were poorly equipped, even—in some respects—subjects for re-education.

I found myself reverting more and more to little children, to the belief that the most important phase of a child's life was the beginning of it. He must be started right.

————————

CHAPTER THREE
TRIAL FLIGHT

TURNING BACK from my fifteen-year-old Pete in the shop toward childhood's beginnings, I came again to the little boy running his railroad system on the nursery floor. I had dreamed of a child world in which railroads and city streets, farms and factories, the stuff of which the real world is made, could be brought down to children's scale so that they might grasp it. I had envisioned a community of children who could in their own way, through the child activity which we mis-guidedly call play, reproduce this world and its functioning. Such a community of little individuals, equals in size and strength and understanding as adults are equals in their own adult communities, would learn not only physical truths about the world, but social truths as well, the all-important truths of people with many individual differences who must live and work with each other.

Certainly this was a harder way to teach children the unity of human endeavor than having them sit in a circle for half an hour at the beginning of the school day. To a tra-ditional educator it was madness to turn children loose as I proposed to do. But to me it was criminal to bind them. I had no faith in mystical circles; my faith was in children.

In its physical terms the plan was simplicity itself: a goodly floor space, basic materials for play, and many children using them together. Out of these modest ingredients I thought I could create a school for little children.

Simple as were my needs, I had to wait until the spring of 1913 before I could get them satisfied. A friend then offered me a small sum of money for expenses if I could find a place to work.

I went to Miss May Matthews, the head of Hartley House, a settlement on the West Side, and told her what I proposed to do. All I needed was a room. I would provide the materials and find the children.

She was quickly responsive to my plan, and offered me the assembly room; but with the stipulation that everything must be picked up and put away at the end of each session. This was nearly fatal: how could any really good play scheme be developed, if we had to destroy it each time and begin from the beginning when we came again? But she was helpless. There was no way she could find to give me the exclusive use of the settlement's main assembly room. Pioneer teachers who are today trying to introduce block play into public-school classrooms—with this handicap among the many they must cope with—may sympathize with my frustration.

On the half-a-loaf principle I decided to make a try. I had thought so much about what I wanted to do that I had to take whatever opportunity was offered to see it in action.

So, with whatever restrictions, I had my floor space. Next was the crucial point in my plan, the materials. Crayons and paper, scissors and paste were obvious. What I sought was something so flexible, so *adaptable*, that children could use it without guidance or control. I wanted to see them build a world; I wanted to see them re-create on their own level the life about them, in which they were too little to be partici-pants, in which they were always spectators.

I knew children yearned to do this, and did it whenever they were allowed, with whatever materials they could lay their hands on. They moved dining-room chairs together to make trains; they set up housekeeping on the beach and baked pies out of sand; they towed coal barges of shingles laden with pebbles. And I had seen children playing with blocks at Teachers College, when the gifted Patty Hill had charge of the Kindergarten there.

She had designed the blocks herself, for the children in her classes to use during their free periods. They were not a part of her teaching program, but I had watched what the chil-dren had done with them during those short play periods when they could do what they liked. To me those play periods seemed the most important part of the school day.

Of all the materials which I had seen offered to children ("thrust upon" would better fit the situation), these blocks of Patty Hill's seemed to me best suited to children's purposes. A simple geometrical shape could become any number of things to a child. It could be a truck or a boat or the car of a train. He could build buildings with it from barns to skyscrapers. I could see the children of my as yet unborn school constructing a complete community with blocks.

But would they? There was something more they needed, a body of information. The little railroader on the nursery floor had evidently picked up information about railroads from observation and experience, and his wise parents had left him free to digest what he had seen, to take it into himself, and then to translate it into physical terms which he could handle. He had been allowed the freedom to gather together whatever he needed to reproduce in his own way what he knew. He was reconstructing a part of his world in which he was most interested.

Just as he had learned to walk and to talk by experiment, he was now carrying his method on to new fields of learning. He was learning about the world, thinking about it, reasoning about it, accepting this, rejecting that, putting it together and making it work.

Children have quite a body of information, more than adults generally guess. I am not talking about information which has been told them or read to them and which, parrot-like, they repeat, to the admiration of the same misguided adults. I mean the information which they have gained by their own efforts, firsthand, often unconsciously. What the groceryman and the milkman bring, what goes on inside the home, in the street or, for country children, on the farm— all this is most exciting knowledge, unless they have been sidetracked by having read to them stories of such sensational content that everything they are familiar with seems tame.

The child is already possessed of a method of learning, which served him well in babyhood. And he has gathered for himself a small body of related information. He needs only opportunity to go on with his education.

That "the proper study of mankind is man" he does not

need to be told. He has been studying it since the day he was born. But he studies it in his own way, by experiencing it with his own eyes and ears and muscles. He makes a train of dining-room chairs so that he can be a locomotive engineer; like his grown-up counterpart, he watches signals and curves, toots the whistle, rings the bell, stops for water, for coal, for passengers. He is himself the train as well as the man who runs it, as well as the whistle and the chuffing steam and the bell, and his performance is accurate and realistic in proportion to his knowledge and experience of trains. He could not make these sounds and movements, he could not feel the imaginary motion of his chair-train in his own body, if he had merely been told about trains and shown pictures of them. But if he has ridden in trains, watched the locomotive come into the station, seen the engineer leaning out of his cab—then, in his play, he can create a train for himself to run. In his play he is no longer an onlooker merely; he is a part of the busy world of adults. He is practicing to take his place in that world when he is grown. He is getting his education.

With this faith in children and what they would do if freed to do it, I went forth into the neighborhood of Hartley House to look for pupils for my trial school. I knew the neighborhood and had no trouble finding half a dozen likely five-year-olds. My choice was carefully made; I had been given only two months for my experiment, too little time to prove anything except with responsive youngsters. Those who already looked at the world with dulled eyes would take a little longer than the time I had to spend with them.

I invited my chosen six to come and play at Hartley House, and when they came on the first Monday morning I was ready for them. There were the blocks I had had made, and toys I had designed and made myself; there were crayons and paper, and there was clay. I had laid them out carefully so the children would not only see them, but could go and take what they wanted without asking. Nothing was out of their reach; everything was visible, accessible, and theirs for the taking. I had planned my display like a salesman, thinking of everything I knew about my small customers: anticipating the short reach of little arms, the tendency of piled-up objects to fall down and frighten a shy child away, the reluctance of a small child to hunt for something he needs. I made it all as easy and inviting as I knew how, and then I stood aside and let them forage for themselves.

The preliminary shufflings and scufflings were suspenseful minutes for me. So anxious was I, waiting for Marjory, finger in mouth, to cry; for Alice and Joseph to come to terms over a box of bright crayons, that I did not see what Michael was doing until he was well started.

Michael had apparently made straight for the blocks, recognizing them at once as just the thing he needed, for when I caught up with him he had already begun to lay out a city street. He built houses, horse-stables (this was, remember, more than thirty years ago!), and brought into his scheme all sorts of things which he had already stored up in his own brief experience.

I couldn't have asked for a more appropriate demonstration of my belief in the serious value of children's play. Michael was so deeply absorbed, so purposeful in his construction, that he might have been a scientist working out an experiment in a laboratory. The likeness was no accident. He was precisely that, on his own level. He was not merely pushing blocks around; he was not even merely learning what could be done with blocks. With blocks to help him, he was using all his mental powers, reasoning out relationships—the relation of the delivery wagon to the store, the coal cart loaded from the barge in the river and carrying its load to the home —and he was drawing conclusions. He was learning to think.

In time several of the other children caught on to what Michael was doing. Although the trial period was too short for all of them to develop such freedom as his, his very concentration made him the focal point of the room. Joseph began to build a house on Michael's street; he who had fought Alice for a box of crayons one day voluntarily handed over a wooden man to drive Michael's coal wagon; eventually they were planning a firehouse together. Marjory gave up crying and got herself a toy. Constructions of one sort or another began to spring up at various places on the floor. Some of the children took more readily to crayons and clay, but all of them were busy at something. Quarrels flared and died, rarely needing arbitration. The work in hand was too absorbing to brook interruption for long.

When the busy minds slowed down and the work stalled for lack of information, we had ways of getting started again. We might sit around on the floor—what part of it was left clear—and discuss, and out of the children's storehouses of memory would come more facts and more relationships. Or we could go out into the street and make our own discoveries about the interesting everyday life around us.

How much those five-year-olds taught me in two short months! With my heart filled with gratitude to them for justifying my faith, I was kept busy checking theory against practice. It was so clearly right that play was learning, that this voluntary, spontaneous play-work was far too valuable to be ignored as our schools ignored it, or relegated to spare "free periods" in the school day, or to the home where a child could work out such play schemes when parents were too busy or too wise to interfere.

Other basic and precious truths became clear. Secondhand knowledge was of little or no use to these children. Words are too recent an acquisition to a five-year-old; his tools of learning, the ones with which he is most capable, are still his own senses. When we thrust verbal information upon him, stories and talk, we are actually coming between him and the things he is trying to learn.

Devoted mothers who spend much of their time with their children in the early years should especially take this lesson to heart. Eager to give of themselves, they make the mistake of telling a young child too much, even in answering questions. Much later in my work with children I learned the truth of the discovery Lucy Sprague Mitchell made: a young child's question is not always meant to be answered. It may be a way to open a conversation; it may be a question to which he himself wants to supply the answer, to verify a recently acquired bit of knowledge. That all children's questions must be answered is a rule with too many exceptions. A better rule is to let the child find the answers himself.

My six little teachers soon showed me I could do better than read stories to them about the things they needed to know. I could take them where they could see for themselves. Later, when the school became established, these journeys in search of firsthand knowledge became a most important part of the work. They became actual field trips, comparable to the field trip of any adult scientist. A question arises in the seven-year-old group: where does the garbage truck take the garbage? A trip to the Sanitation Department's disposal plant is the miraculously simple answer!

During this two-month trial there was no time to go far afield, nor for five-year-olds was it necessary. Their horizon was still quite close to home. But the principle came through clearly. If the child's own play-work was to be his learning method, as I insisted it should, then he must get his inspiration for it in his own way, by knowledge gained with his own eyes and ears, questions asked by him about things *he* wants to know, answers found by him within the limits of his own ability to find and understand them. A teacher or parent or sympathetic adult can help and encourage him in his researches, but the original impulse comes from him.

A really understanding mother understands not merely that the baby wants his ball. She understands also that she must let him get it himself. So with the less tangible things for which the child reaches as he grows older. Encourage him when he needs encouragement, comfort him mildly when he fails the first few times—but let him try, let him do, let him think for himself. He learned to walk and talk that way; it is his own true way of learning.

Just as I could not do the experiencing for the children—they had to do it for themselves—in the same way I saw that

Caroline Pratt's unit blocks
have been used by many-aged
children for many purposes...
for 75 years.

Blocks used on a
large scale, outdoors.

In winter, frozen snow has been cut into blocks by the children—and igloo construction studied.

I could not meet their social situations for them. For my six little teachers were teaching me not only that children can and do learn by play. They were also showing me that children learn to work harmoniously with each other the more quickly and effectively if there is little or no adult interference.

For I was conducting this group without discipline as it was known in schools or even in most homes. The children were really and truly free, even to do battle with each other; I was there to see only that no damage was done. I discovered that Joseph stopped snatching blocks from other children when he found his method did not get him the block he wanted; it only got him a fight. Marjory stopped crying for what she wanted when the wanted thing became important enough and crying did not bring it to her; she went and got it for herself.

John was a problem because he was no problem. He lived alone and liked it all too well. He circled carefully around the other children, uttered no word to them or to me, worked exclusively on his own projects—and very well he did them, too. But such exclusiveness was not natural; children are the reverse of isolationists. Alas, there was not time in two months to pierce the barriers behind which John was hiding; I considered it a triumph when he moved his building out of the corner to within a foot of Alice's.

There would be ways to reach children like John, and time to spend with their problems and the many other problems, the nameless fears and deep anxieties that beset little children —when I had my school. Now, after my trial flight, I was satisfied at least that I had made a beginning in the right' direction.

I foresaw plenty of difficulties in establishing such a school as I planned. Parents would be wary—and why not?—of offering their children as subjects for experiment. There would be the inevitable, deep-seated resistance to anything new. These, and the many obstacles which one could not even anticipate, would be met in good time.

To get started was the important thing. My small taste of success—too small, in time and scope, to be anything more than tantalizing—made me impatient for a large-scale effort. I could not wait to get started.

CHAPTER FOUR

SCHOOL BEGINS

MY GOOD FRIEND Edna Smith did not keep me waiting long. It was she who had financed my two-month experiment. Meeting my excitement over its success with a nearly equal enthusiasm, she proposed financing another trial, this time for a year. I had come to know Edna in our common work for the Women's Trade Union League. Her bent toward social thinking made her an eager advocate of the rights of children, and she was by now giving off sparks on this new venture in education. The money she was able to put into it would carry the expense of the school, and I borrowed the little I needed for my own living.

It is only in retrospect that the high points of our lives rise up, flaunting banners. At the time we have all we can do to scramble up to them, without stopping to survey a misty future from the top. I had no notion that I was starting a school which thirty years later would boast a remarkable body of alumni, a group which would more than justify my faith. It was enough that, after the frantic speed with which my two months had raced by, I now saw a glorious long year stretching out before me, while with more hope than money I set up my school in a three-room apartment at the corner of Fourth and Twelfth Streets. It was the autumn of 1914.

Again I went out into the neighborhood—a different neighborhood this time—to look for children. I have never had any difficulty remembering the children I have known, though there have been so many, but these, who shared with me so important a beginning, have remained with me in fresh, sharp colors through the years. Like Peter Pan they have never grown up, but quite unlike him they are real children, though they remain always between the ages of four and five.

Their parents too are in the picture, and the homes in which they lived, for in this kind of school it is the whole child one must come to know, not just the clean and guarded little face which he brings to the traditional school. Those barriers of fear and hostility which children erect in self-defense against the adult world must be penetrated; a teacher does not say with complacency, as I have heard mothers say, "I can't understand the child." For the mothers I cannot speak, but to a teacher this is a confession of temporary defeat, a promise of continuing effort to break down the wall and free the child so that he can use all his powers to the fullest.

Emily was the first child in the group, the daughter of the janitress in the apartment house where I had rented my three rooms. Her father was a chauffeur and her mother had been a nursemaid; Emily was beautifully cared for, a clean, healthy little girl. Albert came next, his father an Italian waiter and his mother an Alsatian with a broad, homely peasant face; Albert himself, on the surface, had the quick, tough alertness of a typical American city child.

A friendly visiting nurse brought me Katie, a carpenter's daughter, who at five spoke English so well that she was interpreter for her German-born family. Joey's father was an Irish fireman; Douglas and John were five-year-olds of American parentage, children of clerical workers.

Only six of them, but as likely a group as I could wish. They were typical of the neighborhood; in another year they would naturally go to the public school. Their families were poor and could not give them many advantages, but they were not struggling with poverty as I had learned to understand it.

A school, like a home, is where you find it, and to the traditional school it makes little difference what the surroundings are; the curriculum is fixed, though the children differ vastly, and the burden on the teacher is to fit the children to the school.

But the school as I envisioned it had no fixed limits, no walls. It would take shape under the children's own hands. It would be as wide and high as their own world, would grow as their horizons stretched. And as children make use of whatever they can find around them for their learning, so would the school.

Pure chance had set me down on the corner of Fourth and Twelfth Streets with my little beginnings—I had gone to Teachers College only a few blocks away to the eastward. This was the part of New York City known the country over as Greenwich Village, thickly overlaid with the carefree glamour of Bohemia. To people in Detroit or Cincinnati or even as near as Seventy-Second Street in New York, this was an area of bare attic studios where painters painted and writers wrote, chilly, hungry, warmed and fed entirely by their creative urges. Its population consisted strictly of men in berets and Byronic shirts and women with bobbed hair who smoked, all of whom spent their time talking endlessly across wine-spotted tablecloths in odorous little basement restaurants where the spaghetti was cheap. It was all gay, irresponsible, and faintly wicked.

Funny thing—I scarcely saw that Greenwich Village at all, except in the imagination of visitors from out of town. Later I came to know many artists and writers and to be eternally in their debt, for they were my first applicants, the first parents who voluntarily brought their children to my school. Creative people, doing battle in their own lives against the set ways of the past, they were quick to recognize and value an approach to children which would cherish the child's innate creativeness instead of stifling it. Militant fighters for their own individuality, many of whom had sacrificed home and security to follow the call of their own talents in freedom, they had a ready sympathy for the precious individuality of the child. And they were not afraid of anything new merely because it was new.

But I did not know them during this first critical year, nor have I ever, to tell the truth, known the Greenwich Village in which they were the popularly imagined leading actors. For me the neighborhood of Fourth and Twelfth Streets was peopled by old Ninth Ward residents, hard-working members of the humbler professions, street cleaners and plumbers and white collar folk of modest levels, the respectable poor. There was a high percentage of foreign-born in the neighborhood, and as in so many neighborhoods in New York or any big city, its shabby flats shouldered the handsome new apartment houses and elegant private homes of the really rich, the lower Fifth Avenue and Washington Square rich, whose carriage houses, even, were grander than the cramped rooms of my children's families.

No, I was blind alike to the red brick fronts and gracious white doorways (tightly shut) of Washington Square and to the daring Bohemian attic studios. What I saw when I looked down the narrow twisted streets of this old corner of a great city was something quite different from either: I saw an ideal setting for such a school as I was beginning.

There were the great dray horses trotting briskly westward over the cobblestones, the coal wagon rattling behind them, empty. Where did the coal come from, that burned in the grate in our schoolroom, keeping us warm? All we had to do was follow the empty coal wagon. It would lead us to the river, the coal barges; we could watch the coal wagon being filled from the laden barge; we could ask the men on the barge where they got it.

Down the street, sacks of flour were being carried into the bakery, while the baker stood on the sidewalk, wiping his floury arms on his floury apron. My children could not watch their mothers bake the bread as I had watched mine—indeed, as I had baked it myself—but we could go and visit the baker, see him mix the dough and knead it and slide the loaves into the oven.

The pushcarts on Bleecker Street, piled high with fresh vegetables and fruits, would lead us to the wholesale markets only a few blocks farther, and the carts which brought the produce from the freight trains. And the freight trains—in those simpler days—ran right down through the flank of the city, along a cobbled avenue just this side of the river. We could sometimes faintly hear the locomotives chuffing in our very schoolroom, while the sounds of the river traffic came in a continuous counterpoint through our windows.

I could not have chosen a more desirable starting point for our adventures. From our corner of Fourth and Twelfth Streets we could make our journeys, none so long as to tire young children; we could go out to find the answers to the children's questions; we could explore a little way back toward the beginnings of familiar things, not clear to their source, but perhaps far enough for children of this age.

The six children and I spent a great deal of time at the docks. The river traffic, endlessly fascinating, brought good simple questions to their lips, but they were too shy at first to ask the tugboat men and the bargemen and the wagon drivers for the answers. When they saw that I would not do their asking for them they plucked up courage to make the first move, and met with such friendly answers that their diffidence vanished quite away! I helped only this much: I explained to the men that these visits were part of our school work. The men liked being asked to contribute to the children's education; they answered the young voices patiently and carefully. We sat for an hour at a time on the tail of a wagon backed up to the dock, watching the boats coming and going, the tugs nudging the laden scows in and the empty ones out. We saw wagons being loaded with all kinds of things for the city, and asked the drivers where they were taking their loads.

But the mere accumulation of information was not our purpose. We were not training for a Quiz Kids program—or its equivalent of that time or any time, the outpouring of streams of unrelated facts for the entertainment of adults. I have always been deeply sorry for the "bright" child. Most precocity is the fault of misguided adults; an encounter with one of these painfully swollen little egos can give no pleasure to one who has any respect for children.

But to know something and to be able to relate and use that knowledge is the beginning of learning to think. And so, after we had discovered some new facts on our trips, we hurried back to school to put them to use.

Here we performed our exercises in thinking, on the floor, with the blocks and toys. Here the children put to use the facts they had acquired, some by asking questions, but most through their own eyes and ears. Young children are readier to put their thoughts into action than into words. It is a truer exercise for them to push an imaginary barge down a river and unload it into an imaginary wagon than to tell you how it is done. Action is still their medium; words come later in their growth.

At first the children were content with a rectangular block for a boat—to them a boat was a boat whether it looked like one to your eyes or not. But soon some of them scorned such a boat, and labored at the bench to make a pointed bow. And so, as the need arose in the child's own development, he learned to use tools, to reproduce with his hands the shapes he had come to recognize with his eyes. You could trust him, moreover, to select and reproduce the essentials, the distinguishing feature. There was no mistaking this thing with a pointed bow for anything but a boat. If you asked him what was special about the shape of a boat, he might not be able to tell you. Yet the same child would go to the work bench, unasked, and make the shape he could not tell you about in words.

Since the river was so rich a source of information for us, it naturally took a prominent place in the block building. The tug came into its own as the little lord of the river traffic. It towed scows, of which there were many kinds; it helped an ocean liner up the river to anchor or down the bay on the outward journey; it raced back and forth, tooting commandingly, from job to job.

The connections between the river traffic and the city were explored and developed, and the city grew ever more elaborate in the play schemes. But the boats and the railroad trains, radiant with the glamour of movement and noise, captured and held first place in the children's affection; the boys rarely failed to begin their play with these.

So, occasionally, did the girls. But the girls generally, in those early days of the school, clung to their domestic interests. They played mother and children, cooking, washing, feeding the baby and putting him to bed. The only way to extend their horizon was by leading them to see the connection of the home with the outside world. Despite a few rebels, woman's place in our society was still in the home. You needed only to watch the occupations chosen by our little girls, to know it.

Daily, with the growing store of knowledge, the variety of its uses grew. Imagination became robust with the continuous demands made upon it; its lively development was plain to any dubious observer who might have thought that the world of here and now held no stimulus for it. On the contrary, the children's imaginations leaped and bounded, always a step, sometimes many steps, ahead of their building. They visualized a more completed plan as they worked; they developed detail and extended scope; they went back to include functions they had missed before.

As their imaginations developed, they made greater demands on themselves. Hammer and nails, saws and planes were kept busy all day long. The pointed bow for a boat was only a beginning. Carts and drays and even derricks grew under the children's hands. They colored their constructions, reproducing still more vividly what they had seen. You might not always recognize the end product, might not see the fine distinctions between a barge and a cart. But a child knows, because he pushes the one along an imaginary river and the other along an imaginary street. Each makes different sounds from the other, performs different functions. Neither might you recognize the detail of the flamboyantly colorful drawing. But your confusion is yours alone. The children know what they are doing. They are as sure of themselves as the man who reproduces his model from a working drawing. They are sure of themselves *as long as adults leave them alone*.

If I labor the point, it is because I have learned its importance by experience. The over-helpful adult is no help, is actually a hindrance to the child. What perceptive adult has not seen a child's face go blank like a closed door at the very moment when he is receiving the most helpful attention? Who has not had the humiliating experience of having a child walk idly away in the middle of an answer to his question?

I am cross with mothers so zealous that they will not let a baby learn even to walk for himself; I am out of patience with fathers who feel obliged to be human encyclopedias with a complete answer ready on any subject under the sun. To say "I don't know" is surely no disgrace. To follow this with "Let's see if we can find out" is the beginning of an adventure for both parent and child.

Questions came in a steady stream from some of my children when we first began to go on our trips. But when they got their questions turned back at them—"Why do *you* think the ferry has two round ends?"—they were silenced for a while. When the questions came again they were different. They were not asked just to get attention, to make conversation, or for the dozen reasons besides that of gaining information. They were sincere and purposeful; the question now became what it should be, the first step in the child's own effort to find the answer for himself.

Whether I knew the answer or not, I rarely supplied it on demand. Most answers thus given are a waste of a child's time, if not of the adult's. The answer which the child has found out for himself is the one which has meaning for him, both in the information gained and in the experience of finding it. On our trips we found some answers, and some were put over to the future. Open questions are good things to carry around with one; they sharpen the eye and prod the mind; they give the imagination many a practice spin on the way to finding the answer.

The schoolroom saw other activities, too; the children found other ways of dramatizing their lives besides the blocks. "Let's play restaurant," someone would say, and promptly there was a pushing of tables and chairs together, while one or two chose the role of waiter.

The orders flew thick and fast, and surprising orders they were too! "One dark beer ... One ale and a ham sandwich ... Two light beers ..."

"Where did all this come from?" I asked the mothers. Katie's mother was sure the child's father must take Katie to a saloon when they went out for their Sunday walk. She would look into this!

I encouraged the children to tell me "stories"—I wrote them down and read them back to the group later. Albert and Katie, children of foreign-language homes, were the most language-conscious of the six. Albert spoke French, Italian and English; Katie, German and English. Both had seen their parents struggling with the tongue of their adopted land. With the quickness of children at acquiring needed skills, they had even been able to help the grown-ups. Both had unusual vocabularies and a readiness to express themselves in words.

Albert especially found expression in poetic form. Before he left our school at seven, he had produced two or three real poems.

Nor must I forget Douglas, who not only distinguished false from true but was in youthful rebellion against illusion. His parents had given him the treat of treats for a child in those days—they had taken him to the Hippodrome. Far from being enchanted, Douglas was indignant. When he grew up, he vowed, he would burn up all that make-believe. A vigorous partisan of the here-and-now, Douglas reacted to the flimsy "pretend" of the monster spectacles with resentment, as one who had caught people trying to put something over on him.

Yet Douglas' imagination was far from dull; rather, it was independent. He spoke in the poetic imagery of childhood. "The fire is eating up the coal," he would whisper to me, or, "The closet door walked over my head."

Only Emily, of the six, was slow to respond to these opportunities. But I learned from her mother, who cleaned our schoolrooms, that after we had all left, Emily fell to with great abandon. While her mother was sweeping and dusting, Emily had the blocks to herself and made lively use of them. Emily obviously went at her own pace; slower than the other children, she was perhaps confused and rattled by their continuous swift activity. Left to herself, she could work without distraction and was able to catch up with the others in time. I was thrilled one day when Emily told me, "I know where bread comes from: the baker makes it in a cellar down the street, the groceryman gets it from him, my mother buys it and I eat it." Emily was learning to think.

I lost Emily the next year to the public-school Kindergarten. But I met her mother a year or so later, and she told me that Emily had never lost her interest in discovery. Wherever she went, she asked such lively, intelligent questions about what she saw that strangers joined smiling in the conversation. Her mother was inordinately proud of her, and I for my part felt that we had perhaps saved a slow child from becoming a dull one. We had shown her a way to do her own thinking; slow or not, she would be able to find what she wanted to know, and put it to her own uses. She had found her own powers and the confidence to exert them.

I have often thought of Emily when a mother has talked with pride of her child's "brightness." Partly this is unconscious snobbery, partly the wishful thought born of anxiety that a child who is not "bright" will not get along well in the world. Let me say categorically that a child who ranks at genius level on an intelligence test, but who uses only half his powers, is far less able, not to say happy, than an average child with all his resources at his command, organized and integrated, with thinking habits and working methods his ready and familiar tools.

How illusory are those flash talents! The ability to repeat long passages from memory or make lightning mathematical calculations is not, after all, much equipment for coping with the world. It is the whole child we must nurture, not just one part of him. It takes a whole man or woman to live capably in our complex civilization.

My exciting first year was not over when I began to think of the next. When I talked of expanding to two classes, Edna was in full agreement; in fact even offered to take over the younger, mixed group of Fours and Fives in the program I had more or less established during this first year, while I took the original group, now six years old, on into new fields.

The three-room apartment was too small. Helen Marot, Edna, and I rented a small house, entire, on Thirteenth Street, taking part of it for our living quarters and reserving the ground floor and part of the second for the school. Now the school could stretch its muscles a little more; the children could spill over into our living space when occasion demanded. More important, we could isolate a child who needed a respite from the strenuous social demands of this kind of schooling, one who was easily excited or distracted by the group. It was a good feeling, having the physical arrangements for giving each child some of the special attention he needed. Step by step we were beginning to accord each child more of his rights as an individual.

For the third time I went out into the street to look for children, this time with Edna beside me. Sharp on the lookout for four-, five-, and six-year-olds, we were rather a puzzle to the neighborhood. Mothers regarded us with faint suspicion while we explained our program of play. One said, belligerently, "And I suppose a little religion thrown in?" I was startled into laughter—she had accurately measured me as some kind of zealot, but had made a mistake in my creed. I explained as well as I could that my only religion was children, but I failed to get her boy.

We did not get as many children as we had hoped. It was

one thing for parents to send their children to a *play* school before they were six, but quite another to keep them out of public school to send them to us. They were afraid the children would not be ready for public school later, and they were not far wrong. We had no intention of pushing the three R's on the children until we felt they were ready.

But the artists and writers began to come to us during this second year, and we leaned on them quite heavily for the period of the school's development. It took time to become established, to reveal enough solidity so that parents would risk our unconventional methods as against the familiar patterns of the public school. The artists and writers were more willing to take a chance.

For the new group of Sixes we had the same materials, plus bright, attractive poster paints. Yet though the materials were the same, the children themselves changed notably in their use of them.

The block play became a more and more cooperative venture, with elaborate planning and adapting to one another's ideas. So ambitiously did these common projects develop that the group voluntarily suspended work every now and then to discuss them. Presently a group meeting regularly began the day, to talk over everybody's ideas before they went to work on the common project.

I was startled by the memory, at one of these group discussions, of the sitting-in-a-circle practice against which I had rebelled in my brief Kindergarten training days, long before. Here we were, beginning the day by sitting in a circle—more or less—after all! But the resemblance was far less striking than the differences. There was the veteran Albert, trying to make himself heard while the new boy beside him shouted his own proposal, and across the circle they were all yelling at once, so eager was each to contribute. Here was no metaphysical symbol of the unity of human endeavor such as I had rejected. Here was human endeavor in fact and in action, expressing itself in vigorous word and deed, and molded into visible unity by the cooperation of this little segment of human society.

Since the right of the individual to differ from the group is also a part of living in a civilized adult community, no one was forced to join in the group project. A child who preferred to pursue his own plans instead of joining in the common scheme was free to do so. There was no pressure on him, either from the teacher above, or from the group at his own level, to abandon his own work.

But sooner or later—and a finer proof of the wholesomeness of democratic method could not be devised—he ended up by connecting in some way with the group project; the good work was interesting enough to act as a magnet, without any help from outside pressures.

In this group, I found somewhat to my surprise, arithmetic began quite naturally to creep in. The children's activities began to draw upon number work, and with an eagerness to see how far the three R's could accommodate themselves to the children's own way of learning, and how much of them would be in demand for actual use, I went along.

It was in their dramatization of adult activities that the children first felt the need of numbers. They began to play store in real earnest, pushing the tables together to form counters, asking my help in stacking the store shelves with empty grocery boxes of all kinds. And just as they wanted something realistic to buy and sell, they wanted money for the transaction. We began to use real money.

It was astonishing how adept they became, these six-year-olds, at making change with pennies, nickels, and dimes, and how earnestly they accepted the responsibility of handling real money. When we finished playing and had to count up the money to make sure none was lost, everyone enjoyed finding different ways of piling up various coins to equal a dollar.

I would hesitate to confess to my teachers today just how much arithmetic I did put over on these six-year-olds! Actually I went farther than I would care to go today with children of this age, tempted by the opportunity to show

how much a child can learn of the tool subjects when the use of the tool is immediately apparent, when indeed the need for the tool comes before the instruction itself. Children learn eagerly and well when they have need of the knowledge; it was another demonstration of the real effectiveness of purposeful teaching. The drive of the child's own desire to learn carried him, at six, right into the stronghold of traditional schooling; voluntarily he tackled even arithmetic!

Of course some children went farther than others. In the adult world we make no bones about differences in individual capacity. The good traditional teacher tries to take care of the fast and the slow children, although she has to fight her timetable to do it. In our kind of school the right of the individual to go at his own pace is axiomatic, and it is amazing how the more patient method finds them all coming more or less to the same point eventually. The fast ones are rarely fast in everything; they use their extra time to round out their learning. The slower ones catch up in time, very often with a firmer grip on what they have learned than the quicker child, and certainly with a confidence in themselves that they would never have if the pace were forced.

Albert, for example, added fractions of an inch with ease when he was working out a shop problem. In the making of his steam shovel, one day, he needed a bolt to go through three pieces of wood of different thicknesses. He would have to buy a special bolt at the store, but just how long should the bolt be? I helped him measure the thickness of each piece of wood, and he added the quarters and eighths of an inch in his head. Albert had been working a good deal with the fractional measurements on the ruler in the course of his hours at the work-bench, and this problem, when it came up, found him perfectly ready.

Like a parent with a first child, I was inordinately proud to see just how much academic knowledge a child *could* acquire in the course of carrying out his own purposes, and I let Albert go farther than a six-year-old needs to go. Parents who have participated in the growing-up of their first children with perhaps too much eagerness will know just what I felt. They can scarcely wait for the child to grow up, and they push information and experience on him too soon in the excitement of finding out just how much the child will take. When the second child comes along he often has a better chance to develop at his own pace—and so it was with me!

I will say this in my own defense: we kept the numbers concrete. The money we used was in actual coins; the measurements were physical spaces on the ruler and on the wood which a child could see. If a child who used the ruler became familiar with the number symbols as he worked, that could do him no harm. He could always count the measured spaces up to five inches, and the symbol 5 had concrete meaning for him if he did use it.

The leap from reality to symbol, from concrete to abstract, is a tremendous one for the young child, one of the giant strides in his education. A great many difficulties with arithmetic in later years, perhaps even most of them, come from a failure to give children the help they need in bridging this gap. Think of the first time you as an adult were presented with the concept of infinity—have you ever really grasped it, unless you are a scientist or an abstract mathematician? Remember the jokes about Dr. Einstein's theory of relativity when he first gave it to the world; it was obvious that only Dr. Einstein and a handful of men would ever be on friendly terms with such advanced thinking.

Yet when a young child is first confronted with an abstraction like the symbol 5, you might just as well have handed him Dr. Einstein's theory. He can count five fingers on his hand, or five pegs or five blocks or five pennies, at a very early age. These are real things, visible, tangible, concrete. But the figure 5 is quite another matter. It is a curlicue, a scribble on a piece of paper. He can make a hundred of them and they won't·mean a thing. They mean no more to him than the words an adult pours into his ear in answer to a question, the verbal information which he cannot absorb. He can't see it or touch it; it is of no use to him until his little head has grown sufficiently big to hold the symbol as well as the things it represents.

He must take as long as he needs to make this transition successfully—it will do no good to hurry him. Even when he has begun to read the symbols *1, 2, 3*, he should have plenty of objects to count. Toys, rulers, blocks, sticks of wood, marbles, coins, anything he can handle, and count with his hands and his eyes, and separate into groups of different numbers, will help him to fix in his mind the association between symbol and the reality for which it stands.

Even back in Fayetteville I had been aware of this big step in a child's learning, and had used small colored cubes in working with numbers. Now, with plenty of blocks and toys at hand, it was easy to start even with four-year-olds. The six-year-olds used dominoes as well. They became so quick at recognizing number groups at sight that they were soon not content with tamely matching the ends of the dominoes—they invented games which involved adding groups of dominoes and matching those!

So gratified was I at this early and energetic invasion of the realm of the three R's that I had to remind myself, on occasion, of the real work in hand, the children's own work. Academic learning at this age could only be incidental; the buying and selling and handling of money was only a part of the whole drama. The children themselves reminded me if I had been in any serious danger of forgetting; their interest in the whole picture they were creating, the reproduction of the adult world, kept them from working at becoming mathematical geniuses at the age of six.

All over the school, on a rainy day, children were setting up housekeeping, the older children playing fathers and mothers, the younger ones the babies. Family life, father's work, mother's marketing went on in lively fashion. It was a favorite rainy-day game which brought all the children of the school together.

Fair days, however, brought their problem. We were keeping the children all day now, and they needed more than the one or two trips a week to take them outdoors. They needed regular daily outdoor play. We equipped our tiny yard with a slide and a horizontal ladder, which was about as much as it would hold and still leave room for the children. It was interesting to see how they took over everything for their own purposes. They used the equipment for sheer exuberant exercise, but they also used it for their dramas of daily life. The horizontal ladder was less often a ladder than a train of cars, the top of a bus, or an airplane flying through the sky.

Deep as we were in our own rewarding activity, we were astonished to find that other eyes besides our own were upon our work. Evelyn Dewey came to visit the school. She was gathering material for a book of which she was co-author with her father John Dewey, later published under the title *Schools of Tomorrow*.* Her mention of our little school in this book was our first recognition in the educational world.

As a result there were more visitors and some offers of financial assistance. Mrs. Willard Straight came with a friend and spent a whole morning, and the size of the check she sent me later was generous evidence that the morning had been interesting.

Harriet Johnson, then a Visiting Teacher in the service set up by the Public Education Association for the public schools, brought Lucy Sprague Mitchell to visit, and Mrs. Mitchell brought with her a fresh tide of plans for expansion powered by her characteristic enthusiasm.

She offered us financial support. She offered us a new home, a converted garage in MacDougal Alley, behind her own Washington Square home. Best of all, she offered her own services as a teacher, and this was the beginning of a long and rich association.

So, in the third year since we had moved to Thirteenth Street, we were moving again, a group at a time, to Mac-Dougal Alley. The Mitchells' own yard between their house and our new quarters became the school playground. Mrs.

* E. P. Dutton.

Mitchell became teacher of the five-year group. The Mitchell children, one by one, entered the school as they grew, and in time all four of them were our pupils.

Mrs. Mitchell's growing family prevented her from taking full charge of a group for very long, but she taught in the school for many years, and made an outstanding contribution in language work, later also in geography. She made it her task to keep us all aware of the *play* value of language, of preserving the children's spontaneous enjoyment of words and sounds from being swamped by the purely utilitarian functions of language. When we wanted songs and stories that would reflect the children's own experience—for there was little to draw on in the children's literature of those days that had any relationship to their daily lives—she wrote them for us, often picking up a child's spontaneous refrain as the rhythmical pattern of her song. She and the children told each other stories and I think she enjoyed the children's stories with the same delight with which they received hers.

CHAPTER FIVE

NEW TEACHERS
FOR A NEW SCHOOL

THE GROWTH that went on during the next five years, the MacDougal Alley years, was almost intoxicating. After the years of working virtually alone I was all at once surrounded by what seemed like a throng of eager explorers into the uncharted land of childhood. Specialists began to cluster around the school, and their enthusiasm in the new vistas they were discovering had me turning my head in so many directions at once that I felt as though I were on a merry-go-round. I had to struggle to keep always before me the primary goal, that of developing the whole child, not alone any one part of him.

Controversy, moreover, swirled about our heads. A good part of the educational world had been thrown into argumentative confusion by the preaching of Marietta Johnson (a disciple of Henderson, who had stirred up my own thinking years before), Mme. Montessori, and above all John Dewey. Many teachers and would-be teachers, who had been dissatisfied with traditional methods and were newly inspired by these revolutionary approaches to education, came to visit our little Play School and asked to join in our experiment. I had found myself in disagreement with other educators on this or that point, and as a consequence I was often challenged to come out and do battle for my ideas. Perhaps I played a coward's role in refusing to engage in combat. Partly, I confess, I was terrified to speak in public. But my plea that I was too busy learning about children to make speeches about them was perfectly sincere. To spend my time talking when there was so much work to be done seemed to me wasteful.

And dangerous too. All my life I have fought against formula. Once you have set down a formula, you are imprisoned by it as surely as the primitive tribesman is imprisoned by the witch doctor's magic circle. I would not be talked into marking out any blueprints for education, outside the school or within it. This refusal to formulate a "system" made me a problem to our teachers—but more of that when we come to it.

If I had ever thought there was truth in the easy literary phrase, "the simplicity of a child," those years would have taught me otherwise. There is nothing simple about a child; a glance around the room during one of our discussions was evidence of his complexity. There was the physician (Dr. Edith Lincoln), the psychologist (Dr. Buford Johnson); there was music (Harriette Hubbell) and art (William Zorach) and literature (Mrs. Mitchell). We had cooking and sewing and shop and even a specialist in animal life. All this for little children from three to eight years old. And since we had expanded to embrace not only the special branches but so many more age groups as well, there were the group teachers, the core and kernel of any school, and in such a school as ours the most important exponents of our philosophy.

The specialists not only brought their expert knowledge to the school but engaged in eager study of the children, giving us the benefit of their findings. The air was full of discovery, not infrequently of surprise. I remember how one expert's faith in the Binet intelligence tests declined when she found on the basis of her tests of the children from year to year that human intelligence is not after all fixed at birth, that it can grow if given the right kind of nourishment to grow on!

The revelations being made on every hand presently developed into a body of new information about children that seemed to these co-workers and to me to merit recording. Out of this need, and the apparently insatiable hunger of experimental work for financial support, grew the Bureau of Educational Experiments. The Bureau continues its work of scientific study, recording, and encouragement to this day, from 69 Bank Street, where a valuable mass of research materials is kept.

I had long had the arts on my mind, especially music, and had begun some time before a search for a musician who would offer the children in music the same unforced opportunity to experiment as we were giving them in other fields. Harriette Hubbell came to visit the school one day, and remained to carry on for many years this new approach to music. She would go into the room where the three-year-olds were at play, bringing a set of tone bars or some bells tuned to form a scale, and arrange them on a table. She would strike the notes, and first one child, then another would come up to watch and listen, and beg for a turn. Soon the whole group was around her, making their own musical patterns with the bells, matching the sounds with their voices. Singing to piano accompaniment came next. The older children made up their own songs as readily as they dictated stories.

From such beginnings the children and the music grew until later, in the hands of Margaret Bradford who took over, music became a most significant part of the program, with choral singing and not one but two orchestras, junior and senior.

William Zorach was a struggling young artist when he became our first art teacher, and I liked his work with the children especially because he refused to teach. Encouragement and inspiration were what the children needed, as he was quick to see, and these he supplied. Through the age levels the art work began to take form. Clay modeling passed the mud-pie stage and became an effort at interpretation; some children reached an astonishing degree of competence at expressing their ideas of shape and movement. Drawing and painting, we found, also passed the apparently aimless period, in many cases at five years and sometimes as early as four. The drawing became either factual or pure design, and the children made a sharp distinction between the two. As a child acquired a repertoire of objects which he could reproduce to his own satisfaction, he tended to throw them together in compositions which had meaning as well as form. The teacher's contribution might be to call attention to space which could be filled, or to ask, "Where is the automobile going?" which might produce a house or a garage; or "What does the car pass along the road?" which might result in a tree. It was gratifying—we came later to accept it as commonplace—how critically even six-year-olds surveyed their own and each other's productions. Without prompting from the teacher they began to see the work in terms of form, balance, composition: "This side is all empty and that side is crowded, everything all pushed together," or "The man is too big for the locomotive," or "That's a silly boat—it sits on top of the waves. No boat can do that!"

Since we were not interested in turning out young Picassos but only in giving children the freedom of all kinds of materials and media for the expression of their ideas, we had on occasion to discourage these young critics, who were likely to be too forthright for the good of the children whom they criticized. One youngster in the Sevens would not touch paints for a month when the class had laughed at him for painting his locomotive pink! I sometimes feared that if we discovered a genius, his contemporaries would shame him into becoming an academician, such is the conservatism of children.

Occasionally our forays into this field or that turned out to be more experimental than practical. Laura Garrett, who introduced the study of animals, brought in live specimens ranging from frogs to huge snakes. There was a panic one day when one enormous snake disappeared, a valuable specimen belonging to the Bronx Zoo. Quite a different kind of panic developed the next day when he reappeared, coiled up under the desk of one of the secretaries of the Bureau of Educational Experiments!

I was not altogether in sympathy with this method of animal study in which the animals were so far removed from their environment. All the children could observe, really, were the processes of eating, elimination, and reproduction— important processes, but it was life with all the adventure left out. Eventually we dropped the attempt to make the acquaintance of exotic creatures like the big snakes, and limited our zoological studies to smaller and more familiar creatures. Rabbits, guinea pigs, and white mice became regular inhabitants of the science room; turtles took their leisurely way around the floor, and tadpoles grew into frogs in the aquaria.

But this was no substitute for country living, which I for one felt was a serious omission in the lives of these city children. The youngsters whom I had snatched, so to speak, off the streets to make a student body for our school during the early years—the janitor's daughter and the carpenter's son— had no summer vacation in the country; their families did not have that kind of money. So for several years we maintained our own camp at Hopewell Junction and moved the bulk of the school there for two months during the summer. Increasingly, however, the school was sought by families of better incomes who were accustomed to make their own country arrangements for the summer and we abandoned the camp. The name *City and Country School* remains as the only vestige of this early experiment, witness to an unaccomplished ideal for which, with my strong feeling for the value of country experience, I still cherish regrets.

While we, the staff, percolated like coffee pots constantly on the boil with new ideas, the children meanwhile went busily about their work of growing in every direction, unaware that they were the objects of so much searching scientific attention. If they had known, I am sure they would have given our efforts only passing notice. They had so much of their own experimenting to do!

And I for my part was very deeply involved in the search for teachers for the age groups as we added them. There was then no source for such teachers as I envisioned, no training school which could supply me with this most precious kind of material. It is the individual teacher who makes teaching an art as well as a science—not the school principal, nor the superintendent, nor even the educational psychologist, but the person who lives the hours of the school day with the children themselves. Whatever the system is which governs her, whatever the curriculum, traditional or progressive, it is she who must interpret and act upon it in terms of the young individuals to whom it is directed.

And such a school as ours, in which she had a basic philosophy to guide her but no fixed schedule of study, not even a standard of accomplishment which her children must meet by the end of the term—in which, indeed, the individual child determined the course and rate of his own progress—such a school leaned all the more heavily on the resources which she as an individual could bring to the classroom.

It was she who must make the day-by-day, even the moment-by-moment decisions which added up to a teaching method. She who must learn about her subjects—the children—by working with them; she who must frame her curriculum around their changing needs as they developed, both individually and in the group. She who must know how to act quickly in a specific situation. She who must deal each day with such questions as how far we shall push our ideas of order on the children; just when they are ready for short cuts in learning, like correct shop practices, or the multiplication tables; what kind of information they need, and when and how it should be offered to them.

And she it was who met the deeper problems of the child, the problems of emotion and behavior: when to encourage a timid child to fight for his rights, how to meet the lack of security that often underlies unduly aggressive behavior; when to mother a child and when to serve up a little wholesome neglect, and when to step in and take responsibility from the children's shoulders onto her own.

Ideally these are demands which a teacher must be prepared to meet in any system, however fixed by tradition, and the really great teacher who meets them as a matter of course can be found practicing her unequaled art in the one-room country school or in the mechanized stone and cement plant of a great city's educational system. Most of us cherish the memory of at least one such teacher from our own school days. The pity of it is that she is so rare; to rise above the restrictions which are at once an enslavement and a crutch, she must be a great human being, and great human beings are necessarily rare.

But teachers who could bring such creative gifts and such mature wisdom to the classroom were the lifeblood of our work; we could not settle for less. My task of finding such teachers was all the more difficult.

They came, as I have said, from many places to the school, and I went out as well to look for them. There were some who had an understanding of what we were trying to do, but no actual teaching experience. Others, experienced teachers, were sometimes hampered by work habits which were difficult to break through. I tried to make my choices from both groups on the basis of individual maturity and understanding, and I found that previous experience had little to do with success or failure. It was the individual's own equipment which in the end determined her fitness for this exacting kind of teaching.

The fact that I found any to meet the specifications may be hard to believe, but our average of success was encouragingly high. A background of interest and experience in social work seemed to produce the best kind of teachers, perhaps because the same qualities which we needed, of initiative, courage, and warm human understanding, coupled with an instinct for seeking first-hand experience, had drawn them into social work in the first place.

If the task of finding this new kind of teacher for the school was difficult, the next step—that of explaining the kind of teaching I believed in—was even harder. One of the teachers who came through this painful growing period was asked recently by a school parent if I had always been so inarticulate.

"Oh, yes indeed!" she answered.

"Then how did she ever get across the fundamental ideas of the school?" was the inevitable question to follow.

"As I remember it, she gave us all a free hand and then jumped on us hard when we went wrong!"

I dare say this was true. But we did meet regularly once a week as a staff to thrash out together our common principles and practice. Temperatures, if not tempers, ran high during these discussions, but out of them grew real unity of purpose and procedure.

I would say I wanted our curriculum to be based on experiences offered to the children—and so simple a statement as this, simple on the face of it, led to weeks of wrestling with the actual meaning of the word *experience*. "Is a trip an experience?" "May not literature be an emotional experience?" "Is one kind of experience more valuable for children than another?"

The questions flew about my head like missiles, and one day I went home determined to evolve a sort of curriculum chart which would bring out the kind of balance I was striving for, and would serve as a framework for what we were actually working out in practice. I tossed out abstract definition and divided the work categorically into Play Experiences, including block building, dramatic play, art; and Practical Experiences, into which fell shopwork, cooking, care of materials. These two were the core of our curriculum. Supplementary were two other headings: Skills or Techniques, including sense training, number work, language arts, music techniques; and Enrichment of Experience (we later called this Organization of Information), which included such things as trips, discussions, the use of books and stories, all the ways of seeking and pooling information.

I invited the teachers to list under these headings the actual work their children were carrying on. To my amazement it worked. The teachers seized eagerly upon this way of organizing their thinking and planning. They began to keep records of their work under these headings, and to compare notes with each other.

In developing these curriculum records the Bureau of Educational Experiments gave us valuable help in the services of Mary Marot as Recorder for the school. She stimulated and organized the recording by the teachers themselves of what went on in their classrooms, and urged them to write records of the whole group instead of the individual child, as they had begun to do. By showing each child as a part of the group she felt we could more thoroughly describe the social experience of the children, and she was right. The purpose of these records for us was to project something for study, something that would help the teacher in examining her own activities and those of the children. Later some of these records were published and did much to explain our work to the educational world.

Since we believed in concrete experience as the essence of education for little children, it was natural to trust in the same principle for the education of teachers. Very early we began to take into our classrooms as student teachers a few volunteers who wanted to work with us. This was one way of meeting our need for a new kind of teacher—to bring them up ourselves. As with the pioneer teachers, some of whom were college graduates and some not, I tried to choose them for their emotional and intellectual maturity, their qualities as human beings, rather than for academic eligibility.

There was no formal training for these first student teachers. I met with them once a week, when we discussed their classroom experience and the questions that arose out of it. The school was still so small that they shared in staff discussions as well. And then there was the constant daily exchange of ideas and experiences, over the lunch tables, the tea tables, during the tidying up of rooms after the children had gone on—wherever two or more of us gathered there was bound to be a conference, so much did the work absorb our thoughts, so rich a study were the children.

But most important to these student teachers, and a more than adequate substitute, I thought, for an organized course in pedagogy, was their classroom experience, their work with the children themselves. Out of that early group of student teachers came some of the strongest members of our staff. Without them I doubt whether the school would have developed as it has.

Probably no one will ever know who suffered most from my inability or unwillingness to formulate the school's plan of work: the teachers, the Bureau of Educational Experiments, or I myself. My resistance to anything in the nature of a blueprint was instinctive and desperate. I know that I trusted in the school as a living, growing organism to produce something beyond any blueprint if children and teachers and I were all given scope for our own initiative. My greatest effort, it seems to me now, went into keeping this door open, and resisting at every point the fatigue, the discouragement, the fears which would throw us back upon the beaten track.

To work to a formula, set down before the work has reached its final form, is on the face of it not a creative method of work. I wanted the teachers' eyes on the children, not on a chart or table of study. Because I felt this so strongly for myself, I wanted these teachers—who had come to us because they believed in this approach to children, and whom I had welcomed because I believed in them as individuals—to have the freedom to work out their own ideas, to grow in understanding of the children and to plan for the children as they learned from them. This was the only way in which the school, too, could grow in usefulness to children.

So, by common consent, we settled for the simple clarification of the various kinds of experience as I had set it down. This was a practical guide for day-to-day planning and for the recording of the work, and it was all the pedagogical blueprint we ever had. The teachers were left free, each to work out her own classroom procedure, to seek help when she needed it and where she could find it. So intensely creative an effort as this demanded the best that each of us could give to it. It is no wonder we all lived and breathed our work, for hours after the children had gone home and often far into the night.

I am tempted to end this chapter with an extract from one of the early records of a six-year-old group by Jessie Stanton, as an illustration of what seems to me a good pedagogical production. The real production, of course, was not the written record, but the living group.

Before the curtain goes up on the children, however, it is important to notice what the teacher has done to set the stage, and also to be prepared to watch how she steps in and out of the action as the play progresses. Remember that there is a classroom without fixed desks or chairs. The wide floor space is furnished only with movable tables and chairs; open shelves of blocks and other materials line the walls.

The children have been given frequent opportunities to dramatize, not only in their block play, but in acting out familiar experiences and stories of various kinds. Trips to the river have given them firsthand acquaintance with many kinds of boats, and stories have been read aloud to them to reinforce these firsthand impressions.

The story used here for dramatization was a very well known one from the *Here and Now Story Book* by Lucy Sprague Mitchell, based on the sounds of fog horns and boat whistles heard by the children on foggy days both in their homes and in school. It is clear from the description of the play that while the story served as a general outline, all the details were drawn from the children's own observation. This is particularly obvious in Richard's insistence on the way a steamer's whistle should be blown by communication between the bridge and the engine room! Again when Edna undertakes to build a tug without such familiarity, she is unable to carry on. The teacher recognizes her constant appeals for help as a sign that she is having no satisfactory experience of her own, and helps her make a fresh start.

In the following paragraphs one gets a picture of children alive, watchful, drawn together by a common purpose, using all their faculties to promote that purpose. It is an organized experience of a segment of working life in the grown-up world.

"On Tuesday, a rainy day, five children were left in the room while the rest were cooking, and at Faith's suggestion, they decided to play the 'Fog Boat Story.' I organized the play, getting each child to choose a boat to build. I showed them the picture map of New York and they said at once that the narrow part of our room should be the Hudson River, while the wider part could be the Bay.

"Celia and Richard built the ocean liner about which the story centers. Albert made the sail boat, Faith the pilot boat and Marie the coal barge. Tables and blocks were used in these constructions. Edna started the tug boat which was to help the ocean liner from its dock but she appealed to me constantly for help and became more and more impatient and disagreeable, disturbing the others, so I finally took her out and left her alone in the office for about ten minutes. On her return I set her definitely to work on a small sail boat and she built quietly. (She evidently did not know enough about a tug boat to carry out that plan.) Marie, who has been self-conscious in other dramatizations, forgot herself completely in this; she worked hard making clay balls for coal after her square barge was built.

"When the other children came back from cooking, the room was full of the sound of fog whistles and they entered into the spirit of the play. As Meta was the only child who was not very familiar with the story, I asked her to make a bell buoy. She made a mound of blocks and Sonia cut a big bell for her out of paper. She attached this with a thumb tack to a block and moved it back and forth as she sang 'Ding dong, ding dong.' I brought in a small bench from the hall to use as a tug. Sonia seized this and with blocks and colored cubes soon made a satisfactory boat out of it.

"Fred took charge of the pilot boat, as Faith had to steer the ocean liner down to the Bay. The chief difficulty lay in the fact that the ocean liner could not be moved. The children decided to *pretend* that it was moving. Sonia asked for a rope for her tug and tied this to the liner. Faith climbed aboard and was about to start when she realized that the boat had no captain. Richard and Celia stuck their heads out from under the table (the hold of the ship) and said they had to run the engines, so I persuaded Florence to leave the boat she was building and save the situation. She anchored her boat in the Bay when she left it. I put out the electric light which had been burning in the room and this added a final touch of realism as the play began.

"Faith as the pilot blew the fog horn on the liner which said, 'Toot toot, 'tis I!' Richard objected to this almost with tears, so we gave Faith a rope which connected with the engine room and when she pulled, Richard whistled. Each child in turn sounded the whistle belonging to his own boat. The pilot finally left the liner and its whistle was blown more and more faintly as it disappeared in the ocean."

CHAPTER SIX

WE LEAVE
MAC DOUGAL ALLEY

MEANWHILE, as has already become apparent, the school had grown by leaps and bounds; by the fall of 1921, with age groups from three to seven and even eight, and so many special activities to boot, we had again outgrown our quarters. It was at this time that the school moved into its present buildings on West Twelfth Street.

Now was the time for appraisal of the past and planning for the future on the basis of what we had learned. This is not to say that the experimental period had ended—nor should it ever. When we have stopped learning about children we may well consider ourselves fossilized, and retire to a museum. But the MacDougal Alley years had been rich in discovery; we had to pause to take our bearings.

We had confirmed, first of all, a basic relationship between freedom and interest. Freedom of itself was not a value. There was no benefit in freedom to destroy, to interfere with others. Freedom was good only if it meant freedom to do something positive, and that something positive was determined by the child's interest in what he wanted to do. The freest child is the child who is most interested in what he is doing, and at whose hand are the materials for his work or play. The mere fact of being a member of a group imposed certain checks on individual behavior, just as an adult finds he must abide by the mores of the community in which he lives. Discipline for its own sake—an axiom of traditional child rearing—was anathema to us. But freedom for its own sake was scarcely better. Freedom to work, and the discipline of work, both individual work and group work—these were the values on which the children thrived and grew.

They were indeed developing work habits. Their play with the blocks made this very clear. Building a railroad with blocks may look like play to an adult, but to the children it is work. There comes the moment when it is even drudgery, like building a structure over and over until it stands. The discipline of work is as surely present as it is in any adult creative venture. As a matter of fact, it was at about this time that we dropped the name Play School because the children resented it!

Another irksome fact of work is that the worker must take

care of his materials. This responsibility too the children accepted as a matter of course. When huge piles of blocks had to be put away after a week's building with them, you would not have blamed a group of children for ducking the job if they could, or for being very chary of taking them out again another time.

But there are ways and ways of getting a job done. I have watched the Sixes on a Friday afternoon, pushing huge "barges" of blocks toward the shelves, where unloading squads call out, "Come into this dock now!" and the room is full of the sound of boat whistles and the movement of active little bodies, toiling shoulder to shoulder. It helps the spirit of the work if any grownups who are about will do their share of the labor too.

I can never think of this problem of how to stop the play and get picked up without remembering a terrible scene Patty Hill once described to me. When she arrived at a friend's house for dinner, the small son of the family was on the floor with his blocks, utterly absorbed in working out an elaborate building of his own conception. Suddenly his mother appeared from the kitchen, clapped her hands and announced briskly, "Time for supper, pick up your blocks and come get washed!" Like a fury the baffled child turned upon his blocks and kicked to pieces his precious building. Torn without warning out of his world of creative imagination, he just could not bear its loss. The violence with which he destroyed the thing on which he had lavished so much care testified to the depth of his anguish. I wonder how grownups would feel if in the middle of the last act of an exciting drama they were suddenly driven out of the theater!

There is no easy answer to the insistent question of parents: "But what can I do? Doesn't a child have to learn that meal times and bedtime have to be observed, and that some consideration is due to family convenience?"

Of course he does. But learning is painful, even to grownups. I plead only for a sympathetic understanding that will help a child over the hard places. Turn-about is fair play. If we ask him to enter into our world and consider our convenience, are we not obliged to enter into his world, if only to help him make the transition? If this mother had merely taken the time to come into the room, to look with interest at her boy's work, to let him show her his fine building, he would have been prepared to accept with only minor protest the warning that supper would soon be ready and he would have to begin to pick up his blocks. It is not too much to ask us, the adults, to think far enough ahead to warn a child and give him a few minutes to accept the necessity that play time must end.

In the Sixes' classroom on any ordinary afternoon I have heard the teacher remark without special emphasis, "It's nearly time to go home—you'd better put all your cows in the barn for the night and then start to get your things on." Just that little consideration for the importance of what the children were doing, just the opportunity to bring the play to a satisfying conclusion, was all that was needed. The children knew the teacher shared their interest in their play; they showed it by calling her to see how they made their animals safe for the night. Children are different from adults only in size and experience; they need most of the same things adults need—consideration, respect for their work, the knowledge that they and the things they do are taken seriously.

Thus by entering into the child's own world—a world of strict logic, once you understand children's basic premises— our teachers were able not only to gain more and more insight but to arrive at a sound working relationship with the children. In these classrooms the inevitable hostility between teacher and pupils, between adult and children, seemed less inevitable, seemed indeed non-existent except for the few children who brought deeper troubles with them from home. Here the teacher was called upon for extra effort to gain the child's trust and give the parents the benefit of her observations so that they might help the child to cope with his problems.

Far from fearing or fighting adult standards, we found

the children making their own distinctions between their play at being adults, and what they called "real work," which involved grown-up tools and utensils and production for actual use. The six-year-olds took pride in such work, so we introduced more shop work and some cooking and sewing. Cooking especially attracted the children at this age. They began by preserving fruits, experimenting with fruit, sugar, and heat. If they failed they were shown why.

In all these activities boys and girls were given equal opportunities, and generally their interest in one or the other was not markedly based on sex. Occasionally, however, we had a holdout. "T. P." Benton, the son of Tom Benton the painter, was stubbornly masculine when it came to sewing an apron, and when he was told that if he didn't make an apron he couldn't go to cooking, he declared that cooking was girl's work too and he wanted none of it. The group tried to persuade him; some of the children pointed out that their fathers cooked, and very well too—without avail. But when the children came back, not only with good things to eat which they had made, but with books for their recipes printed for them, T. P. was won over. He whipped up an apron in no time at all and joined the cooking classes.

While we were paying all this attention to dramatic play, music, the arts, and the practical arts like cooking and shop, we were finding opportunities presented to us on every hand for the introduction of traditional school work.

Geography had its natural beginnings in the children's interest in their immediate surroundings. The shape of the city became familiar on the map, with its islands and bays and rivers, and they voluntarily made their own maps. Some very impressive relief maps made with plasticine were group projects. We made the children aware of direction, to orient them in their surroundings. They knew when they were going uptown, downtown, toward the East River or the Hudson, and it was a simple step to state these directions as North, South, East, and West. Apart from its usefulness in the preparation for geography, this kind of training has its practical side. A

City and Country child very early knew his way around. One mother even reported to me that her boy of seven, the year after he left us, could take her all over Paris although he had been there only once. With no sense of direction herself, she was quite lost without her youthful guide.

We seized our opportunities where they offered, to prepare the six-year-olds for reading and arithmetic. I have already described how the children themselves became interested in numbers in the course of their play. Words and the sounds of letters in words, we found, could also be interesting to six-year-olds.

The teacher would introduce a game of guessing the names of children or of visible objects in the room from the sound of the initial letter. "I am thinking of someone whose name begins with *Mmm*," she would say, giving the sound of the letter, not its name. The child who first guessed right would give the next name to be guessed. "I am thinking of something that rhymes with *boy*," was the theme of a similar game. The children became alert to fine distinctions in sounds and also learned to enunciate clearly. Later when reading and writing were introduced there was less fear in their presence.

While the techniques of reading and writing were only in preparation at this age, the arts of language were very much present. In fact the whole question of the use of literature with children was being hotly debated in educational circles around this time. A school of thought in opposition to fairy tales arose, and the anti-fairy tale campaign actually broke into the newspapers. Like any new idea, it was ill reported and worse understood, and parents have been asking me through the years, with a chip-on-the-shoulder inflection, "Just what's wrong with fairy tales, anyway?"

Nothing, really, is wrong with fairy tales themselves. Many of them are very beautiful, contain a good deal of homely sense and not a little realism, and are a pleasure for parents as well as children. I have always maintained that good literature for children should be good for grownups too, and the best fairy tales certainly meet this qualification.

But as stimulation to the imagination—which is one of the virtues most ardently claimed for them—fairy tales are more a hindrance than a help. It is the same quarrel of secondhand versus firsthand experience. I have observed children who have read and been read to a great deal, and children who have had little acquaintance with literature but a great deal of varied experience with their own eyes and ears and muscles. The result is inescapable: in any comparison of quality, originality, effectiveness of expression, the unliterary child is the winner, hands down.

The literary child may be facile with his borrowed ideas and phrases, but they are borrowed, hollow, without the vitality of personal emotional experience. A child who has shared an early morning sunrise with the birds has had an emotional experience which the child who has merely read about birds and sunrise can never equal. The child who has had the experience, moreover, will recognize joyfully the description of a similar experience when he comes upon it in literature, and will bring his own contribution of information and emotion to the reading of it. His imagination, stirred by his own sunrise, can play about the writer's version; his literary experience is all the richer for the personal experience which preceded it.

Fairy tales as a literary diet for the young child present him with a fanciful world before he has come to grips with the world of reality, before he can recognize, indeed, the thin line between the real and the fancied. Fairies and witches, magic carpets and wishing rings can do worse than confuse him; they provide such easy excitement that he is discouraged from examining more closely the real world, so tame and familiar on the surface, to find the exciting revelations it too contains. Since it is the real world he must learn to live in, it seems to me we are thus giving him at the start a greater handicap than progressive educators are accused of doing when they appear to neglect the three R's.

Fairy tales apart, the study of literature has no greater appeal to the imagination than the study of a steam engine. One man's favorite author is another man's bore—the measure of the imaginative appeal of any subject matter is the interest the individual brings to it. Conversely, if we may dip briefly into literary criticism, the author himself is more or less effective depending on how deeply he has experienced that which he writes about. Good writers look into themselves for their subject matter. It is only the amateur who writes about things of which he knows nothing at first hand.

Instead of literature being the spur to children's imagination, we have found that it is quite the other way round—it is their imagination which stimulates the creation of literature! A child who has been read a story about a fairy living in a flower is far less likely to turn up with a story of his own than a child who has seen a tugboat on the river. The more closely he has observed the tugboat, the more deeply he has been stirred by it, and the more eagerly and vividly he will strive to re-create it, in building, in drawing, in words. He will not need to borrow the phrases for his creation from literature. He will find them inside himself; he will search them out and put them together, in his urgent need to express a moving experience, and to relive it in the act of re-creating it.

Take, for example, the six-year-old who murmured to himself, watching the river activity from an open pier, "The giant shovel takes a bite of coal and he spits it down into another boat." The teacher made no comment at the time, but the next day, back at school, she repeated the line she had heard and asked the child if he wanted to go on with it. The rest came pouring out almost faster than she could take it down:

The Giant Shovel

The Giant Shovel takes a bite of coal and he spits it down into another boat.
Then the coal wagon comes and takes his breakfast away from the boat.

The Giant Shovel takes a bite and chucks it down into the
    coal wagon.
Then another bite and then another bite until the coal wagon
    fills up.
Then chunk a chunk chunk, away goes the bingety bang
    bang truck.
And then comes another truck and gets some more coal.
Then when the whole boat gets empty a tug boat comes and
    pulls it away and it goes back to get more coal and it does
    that until the end of the day's over.

Or this simpler coal poem from a four-year-old:

> Here is my coal truck.
> It backs up and the coal
> Goes down the chute,
> Goes down the chute,
> Then it clinks and it rattles;
> The truck turns and goes away.

A six-year-old intoned this while playing school the day after
a trip on the Staten Island ferry:

The Bell Buoy

> Ding, ding, ding, 'way in the water deep
> I hear that bell so far away, ding, ding,
> 'Way in the distance of the ocean.
> It tells all kinds of ships
> To not go near that bell
> For rocks are underneath you see
> And that is why we have that bell.

Here are two train poems, the first by a five-year-old, the
second by a child of six:

I

> The train goes up mountains,
> Then down mountains,
>
> And up mountains
> Then down mountains.

Finally it comes crashing into the city.
It goes over little bridges and big bridges,
　　Little bridges and big bridges.
Soon it's in the station.

II

Puff, I go and chug, I go
I chug and chug my way today.
　　Power! Power!
I must take my little train along.
I'm puffing steam—
Tch-tch-tch

This is a very dangerous
Very, very, very dangerous stop.

I puff tonight
And I puff out of sight.

I wanna come in, come in;
I wanna come in the roundhouse.

Those above are full of sound images and rhythms, re-creating with impressive effectiveness the vivid experience or sum of experiences which inspired them. The children dictated "stories" as well, which have a different literary merit, that of idea. The first one I give below was told by a six-year-old while looking at her own picture of a seagull on the waves. The second was offered by another six-year-old in the course of a game.

The Seagull

In the middle of the night the seagulls are sound asleep.
And in the morning when they wake up they look out on
　　the waves and they see a fish and they fly over and try to
　　catch it.
It dives down into the water and gets the fish. And then it
　　comes up again and flies away to its home on the rock.
It eats the fish. It does that each day, trying to get the fish
　　until it is all out of hunger.

The Cloud Fairy

I am a fairy that lives on a cloud.
Rain drops are my parachutes—
Snow flakes are my aeroplanes.
I go back to my castle in the clouds.

The fairy's appearance in this six-year-old's story is proof that we placed no taboo on the magical world. Fairies were all right, in their place. But their place was not to substitute for reality. They could wait while we concentrated on the here-and-now; for children who had a good grip on the real world, the delights of fairyland and its comments on reality would be all the richer. It is no accident that *Alice in Wonderland* is a far merrier adventure for maturer children than for the very young.

One more example, a rather astonishing one, will serve to show with what perception a young child absorbs a real experience, and even more, in what graphic terms and with what robust emotional energy he is capable of giving it back. Six-year-old Robin had gone with his group to see the recent celebrated fire of a trans-Atlantic steamship pier in New York, and this is the story which he dictated to the teacher:

Trip to the Burning Pier

The smoke was smoking so hard I had to close my nose. I saw a lot of fire engines. I saw them putting back the hoses and the ladders. I saw two Hook and Ladders, and I saw some lying hoses on the sidewalk. A lot, too. You couldn't cross the street, because they thought the pier was going to collapse. *They thought!* Two boys were sneaking across the street, but fast!

I saw through the building because there was a fire. I saw a river. The Hudson. The big and strong and healthy Hudson! I bet the fire was tremendous. I bet the flames went so high they had to stop the cars. They did! On the Highway. The steel big West Side Drive. I bet a lot of people watched when the fire was flaming because it was one of the biggest fires on a dock in New York City. I bet the firemen had to stay there overnight in case the fire flamed onto another pier.

If it did, there would be a big hullabaloo or a hubbub in City Hall, of course. Of course, it's way downtown. The Mayor would have to call "Silence" in City Hall or, I'll correct it, Town Hall. If it caught onto every deck, every fireman in the whole N.Y. State would have to come. And all the big ships would burn up and all the rats that were inside them.

The basis of a good deal of misunderstanding of the place of literature in the lives of young children is, I think, a common fallacy, the fallacy that imagination is independent of reality. In much of the talk about imagination the word is used as though it were another name for fantasy.

Fantasy, however, is only one aspect of imagination, to my mind a bloodless and unprofitable exercise for young children. A child whose eye can make a boat of a stick of wood and who asks you to share with him the delight of seeing it rocking on the waves, has leaped far ahead in his imaginative progress.

He may play for hours, day after day, creating a world out of very meager materials, and in this he is indeed showing a very vivid imagination. But not—as adults often suppose—because his play is unrealistic and therefore "imaginative." If he says, "A big cow came up out of the water and wrecked my boat," he may be merely making a joke, provided he knows cows. Or he may be misinformed, in which case it will do him no good to have his mother exclaim with delight over this display of "imagination." What he needs is not admiration for his flights of fancy, which will encourage him to indulge in them just for the attendant excitement, but clarification of his facts. He is imaginative in his effort to assemble and re-create what he believes to be fact; when he is unrealistic, it is because his facts are misunderstood, misused, misappropriated reality. He is handicapped, not helped, by his confusion, and acquaintance with the real world, far from hurting his imagination, will on the contrary strengthen and support it, give it solid nutriment on which to develop.

Every teacher finds children's imagination expressing it-self in different ways. One of our children showed his teacher a picture. She could see nothing but smears of white chalk. He whispered, "There's an automobile there. It is going so fast you cannot see it!"

Another child told this story: "It's about a horn. It was going right down and stamped its feet and then it went up to the sky and flew over the automobile and then it was going down and blowed itself again."

This child got plenty of satisfaction out of his creation, but it was the kind of satisfaction an entertainer gets from the applause of his audience. It takes little effort of the mind to throw together a string of irrelevant facts to make an amusing display, but I doubt whether this is a display of imagination. The first child, on the other hand, was really trying with all his imagination to draw with chalk a picture of speed.

If this tying of imagination to reality seems to be hanging it with fetters, denying it the right to soar in freedom as a miraculous gift of the gods, let me hasten to say that, on the contrary, I am eager to give the child not less, but greater freedom for his imagination. It is his knowledge of the known world which allows the astronomer to explore im-aginatively into the realms of outer space where no human eye has penetrated; which turns the physicist's imagination to the monstrous forces imprisoned in the tiny atom. It is his understanding of man's realities which frees the philosopher and the poet to dream of man's spirit. Far from chaining the spirit to the body, I am asking that we give little children the essential knowledge that will, as they mature, free them from material life. They cannot escape the physical world by ignoring it. They can only climb above it when they have taken a firm grasp of its existence. Then they are indeed free, in the far deeper sense of a man who is a master of his tools and can do what he wishes with them.

If I have seemed to digress from the appraisal of our first five years and what the children taught us about themselves during that busy period, it is because we have had, both then and since, to re-examine time and again our approach to this whole question of literature for the young child. Because we were revolutionary in our disapproval of fairy tales, because we trod warily, in fact, in the whole field of children's literature and frowned on offering the classics of imaginative writing at too early an age, we have had to defend our stand to parents again and again. I am not ashamed to be a propagandist—this entire volume, I rather think, is a piece of unblushing propaganda for the rights of children—and I have propagandized for thirty years for the right reading matter for young children. Later they will become voracious; they will read everything—as I read Shakespeare and the English novelists before I was fifteen—and that is good. But when they are little and at our mercy is when it is important to choose wisely for them. They can be premature little adults, carrying on a kind of intellectual clowning for the amusement of misguided grownups, wearing oversized intellectual clothes to cover a very confused little mind. Or they can be straight-thinking little citizens, with a good grip on reality and all their gifts free to develop—including the precious gift of imagination.

CHAPTER SEVEN

SEVENS—
A GROWING-UP YEAR

THE MOST pressing problem we faced, once established in our new buildings with room to grow, was the program for our seven-year-olds. At six these children had taken to shop work and cooking with enthusiasm. I have mentioned that they wanted more "real work"; the most frequent question on their lips now was, "What do you *have* to do?"—meaning, what do you have to do to get a certain result. They were eager to undertake ventures which had an end product, as in the adult world, and wanted the responsibility which went with it. The Sevens were displaying the first signs of growing up.

Yet, while they scrambled eagerly up the road toward adulthood, they carried with them much of their childhood, like little travelers with their pockets stuffed full of souvenirs of the places they have been. Children do not grow up all of a piece; look for the child of seven, especially, to take many backward glances at the way he has come, while he bounds and leaps unevenly ahead in his growth. These youngsters still had in large measure the "make-believe" which had been so freely exercised in their play and block building up to this time.

As a matter of fact there was a new kind of work ahead for the Sevens. We had become convinced that it was unwise to delay the introduction to reading and writing beyond this age. I do not by any means wish to imply that seven is the biological age for learning to read—I don't pretend to know anything about the biology of it. But since the majority of children do learn to read at six in the public schools, we counted ourselves lucky indeed to be able to put it off for a year, to squeeze in one more year of firsthand experience unhampered by the necessity of learning from books.

Not pressure from parents, nor our own logic, but the attitude of the children themselves forced this decision to give them reading at seven. Public opinion among children is as potent a force as in the adult world. The child who lags in learning to read is looked down upon by his fellows—or thinks he is—and a real feeling of inferiority may develop. Whatever other benefit we might gain, we dared not postpone any longer the attack on the three R's.

If reading was to be the Sevens' big step, my first idea was to find them a teacher who was an expert in teaching it, to make the introduction as easy for them as possible. This meant going outside our own group of teachers who had come through the years of dramatic play with blocks, of trips and discussions.

As I might have foreseen, the play side of the Sevens' lives withered with shocking swiftness under a teacher who had neither experience nor interest in it. More seriously, the reading and writing tended to become divorced from other activities. It was tragic to me to see children who at six years of age had been full of intelligent interest in the work activities of their environment, now being fed chiefly on the puerile content of pre-primers.

Looking for light on the problem, I went into the six-year-old group one day late in the spring when these children were approaching their seventh birthdays. There I saw, as I had often seen before, a play scheme laid out in blocks in dramatic representation of New York City, even to maplike outlines in chalk on the floor to indicate rivers and harbor. The teachers had begun to put in such lines roughly to separate land and water and avoid confusion in the play, and the children had come to ask for them or even put them in themselves, finding them helpful in their city planning. Practically all the children in this group were involved in the joint scheme, each carrying out his separate function, running the boats, trains, stores, homes, fire departments, trolley lines—an amazingly complex, lifelike community.

Reluctant to see this rich activity suddenly cut off in full bloom when they reached the next age level, I had been thinking that the next step might be for them to build such a city in more permanent materials. I proposed this to the children, and they leaped at the suggestion.

Accordingly, the building of a play city became, the next year, the core of the Sevens' program. Lula Wright, the first teacher to carry it out, described her program in the published record, *Experimental Practice in the City and Country School.*

The building of the play city gave three-fold satisfaction: it met the children's demand for something that would yield results and at the same time gave them an opportunity for dramatization of the real, the adult world; it gave them as a group further ways to make use of and extend their environment; and it lent itself readily to the introduction of reading, writing, and arithmetic in ways closely bound to their central project, so that the mastery of these tools need not become an end in itself but could always have an immediate usefulness.

At seven these children had fairly concluded the oral period of their lives. They knew the meaning of adding, subtracting, and dividing, but they knew these processes with real objects; they had as yet no written symbols for the objects themselves. They had no way of recording facts which they wished to remember. They knew that words were made up of sounds, but they had no visual images of them as expressed in writing. They had reached the point where they felt the need for these tools and most of them were eager to learn their use.

Perhaps the best way I can explain how we eventually taught reading at seven is to quote from *The Place of Reading and Social Science in a Job-Centered School*, written by Bertha Delehanty and Sybil May, two of our own teachers, and issued by the Bureau of Educational Experiments.* This extract about our Sevens is by Bertha Delehanty, who taught that group for a number of years with outstanding success:

"In entering upon the teaching of this very difficult technique our aim is to make the approach naturally and easily—to give these seven-year-olds a sense of the meaning and purpose of reading. In so doing, we hope to avoid arousing such negative reactions as boredom, fear, and the type of competitive spirit that centers around achievement for its own sake. Usually a period of about six weeks is given over to what is familiarly called pre-primer work, but which with us is concerned with material that comes directly from the children's work and play interests. Even after books are introduced, in fact throughout the year, the children continue making their own reading material.

* A Bank Street Schools publication, with a Foreword by Caroline Pratt.

"This naturally assumes a sustained interest on the children's part in the activities in which they engage and would suggest the importance on the teacher's part of keeping their interest alive and genuine. The seven-year-olds have a rich and varied program closely integrated with the group's central activity, the Play City, and the recorded plans and experiences furnish abundant material for reading charts. The first reading grows out of the need for class organization. Daily announcements appear on the bulletin board in chart form, in response to the children's questions:

> We go to shop at ten.
> We go to cooking on Tuesday and Wednesday.
> We go to rhythms on Monday and Wednesday.
> We take trips on Friday.

"It is the Play City, however, which furnishes the most satisfactory material, for here each child has a chance to contribute and the group may select the most interesting experiences to be dictated by the children and made into reading charts by the teacher. Some of them are pretty exciting; rescues from burning buildings, strikes at the warehouses, collisions on the river. Some of them are the result of sober reasoning instead of play experiences. One boy, for example, put a water tank on the roof of his building and started a discussion as to how water got up to the top of the tall city buildings. The science teacher was eventually called in to help us work out an experiment and so arrive at a satisfactory solution which was duly recorded on the chart for all to read.

"There is of course daily drill on the charts; and when they have been mastered the children receive copies which have been printed by the eleven-year-olds and which are made into individual booklets.* By the end of the year the children have a fairly complete record of the outstanding events of the city activity.

"In addition to the charts and booklets we usually run a class newspaper which records events of various kinds—dramatic play in the yard, experiences on trips or city news which has not been accepted by the group for printing. The newspaper is made by

---

* The references to the printing of the Sevens' reading matter by the Elevens, and to school jobs point to a later development (Ch. VIII and following chapters). This account represents the program as worked out over a period of several years.

the teacher in manuscript writing on large sheets of unprinted newspaper.

"Toward the end of November, primers are introduced and when the children have acquired sufficient independence, they may spend their reading period in the library, always accompanied by the group teacher or an assistant. A certain hour is reserved for the Sevens and the librarian helps them select books according to their taste and ability and assists them with their reading. A careful check is made by the adults on the reading difficulties encountered. Lists of unfamiliar words are kept and later taken up in the classroom for special study. It is at this time that phonetic work is introduced as an aid to a more independent attack.

"When cases of pronounced reading difficulties occur they are referred to the librarian who is equipped to give special remedial treatment.

"It is apparent that some of the content of the Sevens' reading helps to build a foundation for future social science work. The newspaper items about New York City contributed by the children, as well as information gained on trips, furnish not only reading material of far more interest than the usual primer stories but also the basis for discussion about how people earn their living (and why some don't), how they are governed, what strikes are and why they arise. The discussions of these happenings, and the dramatizing of them in city play, result in the Sevens being better oriented in their own environment geographically and socially than children who are introduced too soon to the remote and therefore less comprehensible primitive civilizations of Indians or Eskimos or ancient pastoral peoples. By the time they are eight, therefore, our children who have played out and read about life of today are ready to play out and read about life of the past. But for the rest of their school life, the approach is first of all through the school job rather than through play. Reading is presented both as a tool which will make them more efficient in their school jobs, and as a means of satisfying their interest in the here-and-now and in the far-away-and-long-ago."

Now the Sevens had become workmen spending much more time than before in the shop, producing the buildings and the bridges and the elevated tracks, the automobiles, boats, trains which they decided were necessary to the Play City. Each child's work thus acquired an element of responsibility to the group.

The same group responsibility became apparent in the play jobs which the children undertook in the running of the city. If a child who had chosen to run a grocery store failed to carry out his part of the plan, the rest of the city had to go without food, and the inhabitants made themselves heard in no uncertain terms. Sometimes it happened that the grocer found himself engaged in other work at the time set aside for play in the city. But he generally managed to provide a substitute for his job in the city. A neighbor who had charge of the fire department close by might agree to tend the grocery store between fires. Often signs would appear over store doors telling customers where to go in the absence of the proprietor. So the children worked out, over a period of time, a common understanding which combined acknowledged responsibility to the group with individual freedom of action.

Naturally the program was not completed in any one year, nor in any crystallized form. It has shown itself capable of great variation. Some groups of children have run a much more organized city than others; sometimes the city has definitely been New York, sometimes more vaguely "any city." Often it has included surrounding farm life to satisfy children who have come back from their summer with a strong attachment to the country; some have found refuge in "a farm across the river" as an escape from intensely cooperative play which they were too shy to join. How such a child may eventually be drawn into the group play is revealed in the following episode from Miss Delehanty's record:

"Florence was a shy little Spanish-American child. She spoke with a decided accent, and, because of the ridicule and impatience she often aroused, developed the habit of withdrawing from the group into solitary play. Her choice of 'a farm in New Jersey' was based, no doubt, as much on this desire for withdrawal as on the firsthand experience of farms she had had the previous summer.

"One morning during group discussion I said to Florence, 'Tell us about your farm; what do you raise?' 'I have cows and chickens and pigs. The farmer milks the cows early in the morning and at night too.'

" 'And what happens to all the milk? Does the farmer drink it all?' Florence hesitated, and Nancy said, 'The farmer sends the milk from the farm to the station and then to New York.' Andrea added, 'The trucks come from the dairy to get the milk when it gets to the city.' Peter: 'It comes in early in the morning on the milk train.'

"Then I said to Florence, 'Does your farmer send the milk to the city?' 'Yes.' 'How does it get there?' 'It could go by truck through the tunnel.' Carl: 'Or you could have a boat to take it across.' 'And where does it go when it gets to the city?' Rae: 'We should have a dairy.' 'Well, Florence,' I said, 'if you're not too busy on the farm, couldn't you run a dairy too?' Florence accepted the suggestion and in the play period that followed, she carried on a nicely related play carrying milk from farm to city and building a dairy for a receiving center. Nancy and Carl were both drawn into her play. I heard excited voices at the farm. Florence: 'Oh gee, I've got some good news; there are two baby calves—oh, the pigs have babies too!' Nancy, who had a book store that did not hold much interest for her, was attracted to the scene and soon the two girls were playing happily together.

"Florence: 'You milk the cows, Nancy, while I feed the chickens.' Nancy: 'Whee! What a lot of milk! We'll have to sell some. Get the truck.' Just then Carl came along with a tugboat. Nancy: 'Hurray, we're going to get a boat. I think I'll take the milk over and some cattle too.'

"Peter, with his eye on the proceedings, gets some chalk and indicates the water more clearly, saying, 'Here's where the Hudson River runs into the Bay.' Nancy loads up the boat and starts off. Suddenly she cries out, 'There's a storm coming up. The waves are terribly high. Help! A cow fell overboard!' Florence joins in, 'Help, rescue the cow!' The cow is finally rescued and the boat proceeds safely to land. After this dramatic episode, the milk is taken to the dairy for distribution.

"In this way Florence was drawn into city play without having to relinquish her farm, in which she had a genuine interest. It helped considerably in establishing a happier relationship with other children. The very next day, in fact, the farm came into focus again. Andrea, who was running a school, was looking about for a suitable trip for her children. She approached Florence asking if she might take them for a visit to the farm. Florence was delighted with the idea and suggested they bring their lunch and spend the day. Carl's tug was chartered and the group embarked. Florence's farmer met them at the dock with a wagon, and upon arriving at the farm, organized a sight-seeing tour through the buildings, barns, yards, and into the dairy, where a demonstration was given on milking cows. At the end there was a swim in the pool and lunch under a tree.

"Encouraged by the success of this venture, Florence announced the following day that there would be a horse show at the farm. 'Like the one I saw at Pittsfield last summer,' she said. This seemed to me just what Florence needed, an opportunity to relive her own experiences and also to add to her prestige in the group by an acceptable contribution, so I was prepared to push her plans in case her idea fell flat as so often happened. But this time I was not needed. The idea produced as wholehearted a response as Florence could have desired. 'Let's have it now,' someone said and there was a rush for the city.

"Business in the city that day came practically to a standstill. Stores, markets, banks and post office were closed and soon every possible means of transportation was in use, moving the people to the festive scene. Boats, perilously overcrowded with the little wooden 'people,' crossed the river and a steady stream of traffic moved over the bridge and through the hastily constructed tunnel. 'It looks just like Sunday or a holiday in the city!' Lois said."

The greatest change from my original idea of a city built in permanent materials came about when we put in charge of the Sevens a teacher who had come through the younger groups in the school with experience in the use of blocks for dramatic play. She was worried by what seemed to her a void in the program during the somewhat prolonged period when the children were waiting for the first buildings to come from the shop for use in the city play. Either the shop products suffered from superficial, hurried work, or the play lagged for lack of materials, so she asked the children if they would not like to have blocks to use until their permanent buildings were ready. In fact I am not sure the idea did not come from the children themselves. At all events, the whole group went off to the cellar, where some abandoned, well-worn blocks had been packed away, and came back triumphantly with a complete outfit.

So we found again, as so many times we had found, that the children themselves were our best guides to what they needed. The city began in lively fashion from the first week, with blocks. Nor did the Sevens of that year or later years ever completely abandon the blocks in favor of permanent buildings. Meanwhile, work was begun on the permanent buildings by the children in their shop time. With high excitement, building after building came into being. Stores, dwellings, garages, banks—most of the adjuncts to city living finally appeared and were set up. Like all cities, this one was never completed. Buildings were torn down and replaced, new streets were added, and not only an electrical system but even a city water supply has been installed, though in the interests of our school building the water system was carried no further than the demonstration stage!

An unanticipated dividend in the use of the blocks by the Sevens turned out to be its value to newcomers in the group. Children who joined us at this age from other schools, who had never had the opportunity to work with these adaptable materials, often became so engrossed in block building that they scarcely knew what was going on about them. Seven-year-olds, standing as they do at the transition between childhood and pre-adolescence, often suffer from insecurity, and the plunge into an integrated group working with furious intensity at their cooperative project, difficult at best, is even more difficult at seven than a few years earlier or later. We have seen the blocks lure a small stranger first into an absorbing task of construction by himself, and gradually into taking part in the work of the city itself, so naturally that he scarcely knows he has joined the group until, with a burst of confident realization, he has found himself there.

The blocks have been a guide, too, to the teacher in estimating the young newcomer's readiness for the more serious work the Sevens have to do. She has been able to judge, for example, whether he is ready to attempt a permanent construction, or needs more time to experiment with the blocks. Such an absorbing interest as the blocks has very often served to steady a seven-year-old's emotional reaction to his new situation, and free him for happy activity within the group.

Every week or two the whole city was picked up and started fresh. This was perhaps the most valuable part of the program, as it developed. It gave the children a recognized interval for bringing to the project new information which they had acquired in trips and discussions through the previous days, for the avid gathering of knowledge never for a moment stopped. And it gave them, at each new city's beginning, an opportunity to change jobs.

This was of enormous importance. A seven-year-old child who has chosen to run an apartment house and has been busily making one in the shop, will not be able to maintain interest in this particular play indefinitely. It is up to the teacher to rescue him from his self-imposed task before he tires of it, and so the Sevens' teachers have made a point of suggesting that they all try to make buildings which can be easily converted—from a dwelling to a store or a fire house —by a few simple changes of fittings when the owner wishes to change his job. This kind of planning, plus a liberal use of blocks, a very free exchange of one another's buildings and constructions, and the opportunity to tear the whole city down every so often and build it all over again, solved the problem of fatigue and kept interest in the city high until the very last day of the school year.

All teachers are aware of the short span of a young child's interest. The usual answer to this in schools is the use of many short-term "units of interest." The trouble with this solution is that it accepts the situation and does nothing to correct it, offers no help to the child to lengthen the span of his interest and concentration. We found that the child does not tire of the subject as a whole but only, as a general rule, of the particular activity he is engaged in. So, instead of short specialized units such as the Milk Industry, or Fire Protection, or the Post Office, we have offered the children, in the dramatization of a whole city, a wide frame of interest embracing an almost endless variety of related activities. Change and growth are constantly possible within its scope, and there is a constant awareness of the relationship of each child's activity to the whole. Instead of being scattered by a dip first in this subject, then in that, the child's attention is in this way deepened in a single large subject, and widened to include a growing number of related activities. All those specialized "short-term" units and more may be included in a Play City as the children's information grows, and all the activities function simultaneously as they do in real life.

The Sevens' trips in search of information became more frequent, more extended, and more purposeful than they had been in the earlier years. More often than not a trip was motivated by an actual problem which arose during construction of the city. A simple question about bringing electricity into a house led to a trip to a powerhouse, and firsthand acquaintance with generators, dynamos, and more particularly with the men who looked after the city's electrical system and could tell the children what they wanted to know. Some years the Sevens have become so electricity-minded that they have installed most elaborate electrical systems in their city which actually worked, and a mighty pretty sight too. How far each group is able to go along such a special line as this depends entirely on the interest shown by its members, and some groups go a good deal further than others.

Even more important than the acquisition of information were the situations the Sevens encountered as they went about the city in search of knowledge. It was no accident that they came upon parades and mass meetings and picket lines, and returned to school to discuss not only garbage disposal or meat packing, but economic and social problems of far greater complexity. These manifestations are part of the life of the city, and our little explorers into the life of the city were bound to come upon them.

One group of Sevens, going through the neighborhood of City Hall, saw near the building a milling crowd of people held back by a cordon of police. What were those people doing? they wanted to know, and their teacher suggested that they ask someone in the crowd. Finally one of the bolder children tugged at the coattails of a man in the crowd and asked him to explain. The man came over to the children and told them that the people wished to see the Mayor about something concerned with their rights as citizens and that the police were preventing them from doing so. They had tried to communicate with the Mayor in other ways, and finally came to a mass meeting outside the City Hall to call the Mayor's attention to their problem.

Here was a lively field for investigation! They had to know about the Mayor, the City Councilmen, how they got their jobs and what they did. They had to find out what were a citizen's rights and what those rights had to do with the city government. Such a course in civics as these children gave themselves as a result of that mass meeting could never have been served up to seven-year-olds on a teacher's initiative. And I am certain not one of those children has since forgotten what he learned about his city's government at the urgent prompting of his own aroused curiosity.

Yes, that drive to learn—which I had counted on in children from the very beginning of my work—kept the Sevens very busy indeed. What they did not encounter on their trips they brought in individually for discussion. One of them reported to the group one day on new playgrounds which had been opened on the lower East Side. The boy had heard his father read an article about them at the breakfast table. The Commissioner of Parks, Mr. Robert Moses, had told in an interview how ample the playgrounds were, what games could be played there, and how even little children were provided for. The report stirred the class to such interest that they decided to write to Mr. Moses and express their appreciation of what he was doing for children. There was some hope, too, that he might be induced to establish similar playgrounds in our own neighborhood. A very appreciative reply came from the Commissioner, and in due time Washington Square blossomed with modest playgrounds equipped with sand pits for the very young children. Whether the Sevens' letter had any influence with Mr. Moses in this case or not we never discovered, but they had done their duty as citizens, far better, indeed, than most adult citizens ever do.

With all this budding social consciousness, there was somehow still time in this full program to continue the work on the three R's. Arithmetic came quite naturally into the Sevens' lives. They handled real money in making purchases at the school store, and in paying carfares on their trips; they helped the teacher write up the class accounts, a perfect opportunity for drill which included even decimal notation, because the accounts were kept in columns of pennies, dimes, and dollars. Written numbers appeared spontaneously in the city on street signs and automobile license plates. And toy money was used constantly in all kinds of transactions: paying rent, buying groceries, car licenses, theater tickets; paying fares on busses, boats and trains. Banks came into existence, and many seven-year-olds learned with surprise that money had to be put into a bank before it could be taken out. And finally the children made a very serious consideration of setting realistic prices for the merchandise and services they were constantly exchanging in their city, so serious indeed that the mere matter of prices was often a subject for discussion and investigation.

Through the years parents have constantly startled us with the question, "When is my child going to begin to learn geography?" It is a curious idea that children do not learn unless they are taught. Actually these children had been learning geography of a kind even before they entered the Sevens. They were making a kind of map on the floor of the Sixes' room with their chalk marks for the Hudson River and the East River and Upper New York Bay. They knew where they were in relation to their homes and the places they visited on trips. It was a short step to transfer this floor map to paper. A look at the city from a high building, an airplane photograph on the wall of the schoolroom which they studied eagerly, finding their own neighborhood and familiar buildings on it—with children accustomed to paper and paints for expressing their ideas, maps came naturally. Painting a map is not unlike painting a picture, and indeed the Sevens' maps were usually alive with boats and bridges and buildings, painted in very decorative colors.

Cooking, which shared with shop the respected designation of "real work," became an achievement with the Sevens. They went from simple operations like applesauce to experiments in baking, and when they brought home their delicious home-made bread the parents refused to believe such little children had produced it. But the cooking teacher—who did not, like the settlement-house cooking teacher I have mentioned, think of children's learning as "wasteful"—has always firmly pointed out that no one, after all, has seen the failures which came before.

Dressing up and make-believe, so natural a form of children's expression, became with the Sevens a dramatic production. The theater was part of their city from time to time; a small group of the children might put on a play with the "little people," as the wooden inhabitants of the city were called, for actors, and the rest of the city would throng to the toy theater. Sooner or later, the whole group would engage in producing a play, evolving a simple plot, asking the help of the rhythms and music teachers in working out dances, songs, and incidental music. They made the costumes and painted the scenery themselves, and invited the Sixes or the Eights to the performance.

One of the most charming I remember was nothing more than the representation of a snow storm in the city. There were two scenes with backdrops painted by the children on

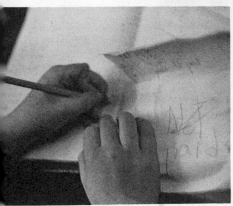

Real jobs involve responsibility
to the school community—
at the store, printing, and
working with the younger children.

Jobs lead to study...

large sheets of brown wrapping paper. The first showed the New York waterfront without snow; the second reproduced the same scene, but covered now with deep white drifts. In the first scene the children were snowflakes, improvising their own dance and finally falling to the ground. In the second scene, workmen came with snowplows and opened up the streets by pushing the fallen snowflakes aside. That was all there was to it!

And then there were the quiet times in the Sevens' room, the times when each child turned to some interest of his own. Far from insisting that all activities be group activities, we encouraged individual expression. They painted or drew or modeled with clay, dictated—later, wrote—their own stories and songs, went to the library to read for pleasure. And what an exhilarating experience to go to the library shelves and pick their own books for the first time—the librarians made a point of arranging the shelves so that even such new readers as the Sevens could choose for themselves.

And so, with the guidance of the children's own interest, we evolved for a difficult year a full and rich program. In this important period of transition, the school day full of a variety of work which held their attention and commanded their respect was what they needed to carry them through childhood to the responsible years. Life became to them more like what it seemed to be for grownups, and they were supremely satisfied.

CHAPTER EIGHT
THE EIGHTS TAKE A JOB

WHILE THE Sevens had thrived mightily on the return to blocks, had indeed used them as a steppingstone to large new vistas and brave undertakings on the way to growing up, with the eight-year-olds, alas, it was not so at all.

The Eights loved to be turned loose with blocks on occasion—but for them the fun of building quickly deteriorated into a return to infantile skittishness and ended sooner or later in bickering and even battle. They were showing us in every unconscious way they could that they were ready now to put away childish things and buckle down to grown-up work. What they needed, they told us as plainly as they could without words, was a job.

At least this was our conclusion. We were determined to learn from the children at every point, to keep our eyes fixed on what they did spontaneously, outside of school when they were free of adult domination, rather than slavishly to follow what had been set up as proper school procedure. We put the two and two of our observations together and interpreted the result to mean: a job.

Perhaps I remembered my own passion to set up a lemon-ade stand on the village street in front of our house, or to give a show and charge a penny admission. Certainly, like every-body else, I had seen this going on among children of about this age. Any skeptic can look into his own past for corrob-oration. Parents for generations have been quick to take ad-vantage of this yearning on the part of eight-year-olds to do honest-to-goodness work. It is at eight, or thereabouts, that we began to be little helpers—we dried the dishes, hauled the wood, fed the chickens.

But there was a rub to it. We always got the mean end of the work, the tasks that were distasteful to grownups—and how much more so to us! We were called in the middle of our games to run errands. We scraped the carrots, peeled the potatoes. My elder sister resigned from the cleaning of the lamps when, as I look back on it, I was still an infant.

We would have been willing enough to wash our own dishes if we could have made cookies or muffins or cake. Even cleaning the lamps would have made sense to us if we had been allowed to stay up and make use of their light. But cook-ing would have taken some teaching, and we would have wasted food and made messes in the kitchen. Dishes and lamps could be thrown at us without any loss of adult time—

we could be left to sink or swim in dishwater or kerosene oil.

For the sake of all the glum little lamp-cleaners and errand-runners of the past, I was determined that our Eights should have a whole job, with the adventure of planning and the glamour of accomplishment, no less than the necessary drudgery which is a part of all work. And the job must be real. It must be of actual service or the essence of it is lost. Eight-year-olds were through, for practical purposes, with the make-believe of childhood. They were ready to try their powers on the real world.

The suggestion that they be given a school store to run came from Nell Moore, who was then their teacher. She had watched the children *play* store and knew that they were interested in the processes of buying and selling. Moreover—and here we see again that a fine teacher is not necessarily one who has had the most complete pedagogical training, but one who has had experience as a human being and is creative enough to take advantage of it—Nell had herself worked in a department store, and was impressed with the possibilities for learning in an actual commercial activity. These children were not fluent readers and had done very little written arithmetic. They could, she pointed out, learn these techniques through their interest in buying and selling school supplies. Most teachers would have swallowed hard at such an undertaking, but not Nell Moore. She saw a hard term ahead, I am sure, but we could not have stopped her from trying if we had wanted to.

The first requirement of a job for children—that it have real usefulness—was certainly met by this one. The office was having trouble with supplies. They were kept in an inner supply room, and although a specified time was set aside for their distribution, when the children came in for their stocks of paper and pencils and notebooks the other work of the office had to be abandoned. The office force consequently welcomed the Eights with enthusiasm. But the real enthusiasts were the Eights themselves. Their whole approach to their job was so eagerly and intelligently constructive, and they were so willing to undertake whatever dreary tasks might be necessary in connection with it, that we felt we were heading down the right path. If we could only maintain half this initial surge of interest our problem was solved.

First came a considerable job of physical planning and serious carpentry. A corner of their classroom which had a window opening into the hall was partitioned off for the store. The window sill with a table behind it served as a counter, and they lined the walls of the store corner with shelves for the paper, pencils, drawing paper, crayons, thumb tacks, paints, brushes—the many items which an elementary school needs as it goes about its business of education.

They decided that they had to have money to lay in their supplies. Like a proper business venture, they borrowed a sum of money from the office, which acted as their bank, and bought at wholesale prices the supplies the school had on hand. They added to this stock with the cooperation of a wholesale house which agreed to help them by supplying small quantities at a time at the same rate, and holding the stock for them until called for. I have always been impressed with the quick response of workmen and businessmen when we have called upon them for help in the children's learning. They have seemed to know instinctively, with only a minimum of explanation, that what these children were doing was right and good. Stevedores and printers, small shopkeepers and owners of factories have been eager to help the children in their quest for firsthand knowledge. And so it was with this wholesale stationery firm; whatever inconvenience it might entail to do business with a group of eight-year-olds, they were willing to go along with us in our effort to give the children this experience.

Even after the Eights' store was set up and open for business, the venture was constantly improved by new ideas from the children. Trips to outside stationery stores gave them suggestions for caring for their stock. Eager volunteers toiled in the shop at stools for the clerks to sit on, a cash box, a step-ladder for little salespeople to climb to upper shelves, a sectional box for paint brushes of different sizes, and even a fine desk with drawers for the cashier.

Nell Moore, up to her ears in the mechanics of setting up the store and getting it running, found the creative energy somewhere to watch at the same time for every opportunity to make the store teach the children. Reading, writing, and arithmetic became urgently needed skills to the little store-keepers.

First there was the list of all the supplies for sale, and their prices—every Eight diligently made copies and distributed them about the school, while a large price list was posted in the store itself for the children to refer to.

She showed them how to write their sales slips in duplicate, and this proved to be the most realistic touch of all. The children never tired of practicing on these regular commercial pads with carbons, exactly the same as those used in grown-up stores. The examples they used in arithmetic drill were the very ones they encountered in the store. They all but devoured their multiplication tables. There was no need to point out the necessity for these short cuts; it was plain to anyone with eyes and ears, who could see and hear the clamorous customers at the store window waiting to be served.

If an individual child was slow to see this necessity the group soon put him right. One little girl was so slow in making out sales slips that she held up the customers until they became critical, not to say abusive. Her small partners in business found that she did not know even the simplest of the tables, and they took away her job until she could make good. She learned some of the tables overnight.

It is well to remember that many eight-year-olds have little impulse of their own to read or write or use numbers. So far as they are concerned—barring the social pressure of other children's knowing something they don't know—they could manage well enough without these accomplishments. But the store had an irresistible glamour, and wrapped up in it was the *need* to read supply lists, to write sales slips, to keep accounts and balance books. If you could not do these things you were not only a social failure—you couldn't have the fun of working in the store! Shop work, modeling, painting and drawing, so agreeably easy by comparison, had no appeal to compare with the urgency to learn the answer to *four paint brushes at six cents each*, or *five cents for an eraser plus seven cents for a notebook!*

The store was open for half an hour every morning, with a rotating committee of children in charge, consisting of a cashier and two or three clerks. The job of cashier was of course the pivotal one, the one the children had to work up to. The cashier made correct change for customers, entered all the items with prices from the sales slips into the book, and at the end of the store period balanced this total with the actual cash received. The word *received*, by the way, one of the trickiest in the English language and a stumbling block for many a college graduate, is one which City and Country School children almost never misspell. It is almost the first word they learn to write.

The cashier, to be sure, was the star performer of the store's team, and while a good deal of teacher's help was needed at first to make the balance match the cash at the end of the store day, many of the children mastered the job during the year and were able to help the slower learners. All the children, however, had the important responsibility of handling the materials and the money, of writing sales slips and totaling them, and of sharing in the functioning of a business venture.

Each week the books were balanced for the week, and each child made out his own balance sheet. The cashier for the week stood at the front of the room, reading aloud from his book the total sales for each day, and the children wrote the amounts on their own papers, totaled them, and added them to the balance carried from the week before. The class treasurer then read in the same way a list of the week's expenses; this in turn was totaled and subtracted from the receipts to find the balance on hand. The teacher meanwhile wrote on the blackboard as an aid to children who found the form of a balance sheet difficult, and difficult indeed it is for most eight-year-olds! Sometimes the sheet took a lot of going over before everyone arrived at the same result.

But then came the exciting moment of actually counting the cash on hand to see if it corresponded to the paper balance. Here was no question of asking the teacher or looking in the back of the book for the correct answer. The proof of this pudding was most definitely in the eating.

In a manner of speaking, they did eat it The moment when the sum on paper and the money in the cash box came out even became such a high point in the week's achievement that the children asked to celebrate their success, when they were successful, by bringing their lunches from the school dining room to their classroom and having a private party. There was one Friday I remember very particularly. The balancing had come out perfectly for several weeks in succession, and the children had developed such confidence that on this Friday one of the girls had brought to school a cake of her own baking to add to the festivity. Only the teacher felt any anxiety over the possibility of a failure.

But when the cash was counted, one penny was missing! There was the cake in its box, almost too great a temptation to eight-year-olds—but not one child in the group suggested that a penny didn't matter, that they could eat the cake anyway. They arose in a body and swarmed into the store to search every cranny; someone ran for a broom to sweep the floor. Sure enough, they found the wandering penny, brought it back triumphantly to the cash box, and sat down to enjoy their party.

The store required a good deal of hard labor outside the daily half hour when it was open for business. Paint jars had to be filled from the large quart jars bought at wholesale; paper had to be counted and done up into packages of tens or fifties in readiness for the customers; shelves and showcase— yes, there was one—seemed to need constant putting in order. Posters or letters to the groups were needed every so often, announcing special sales or changes in prices. Business letters had to be written, bills paid to the wholesale concerns, bills sent out to groups which ordered by mail, and mail orders had to be filled. This last task was a perfect opportunity for slower children to get their practice away from the confusion of sales over the counter.

Practice in any case was sought by the children themselves. A first-time cashier would ask the teacher for a little private practice before going into action in the store. And the teacher watched constantly for signs of nervousness over any part of the job, and volunteered private assistance to build up confidence.

Buying for the store was still another and most important job. Two different children each week took the job of buyers, going with a student teacher to do their shopping at the wholesale stores. With permission from home they were even able to go by themselves, and acquitted themselves most creditably both in their buying and in the going and coming. Most parents of eight-year-olds were astonished to find that their children were so reliable when they were really relied upon! They even learned to save time by using the telephone, giving their orders clearly and explicitly. If they had not done their work so well our wholesale firms would have protested in sheer self-defense, but there was never a protest.

They were mighty proud of their store. Unbidden, they scrubbed shelves and counter, and in an excess of zeal were even known to scrub the floor, although the cleaning man had already done his best on it.

There has always been an unexpected dividend or two from a successful project: in this case it was the curious effect of the store in spreading responsibility throughout the school. Each group now had to have its own spending money, which the office made over to it from a fund the parents pay to cover supplies. Each group had to account for expenditures before more cash could be drawn from the office. Consequently each group had to do a certain amount of bookkeeping. For the younger groups the teachers kept the accounts, but the older ones each had its own treasurer, who served a week at a time. If the treasurer was slow or inaccurate the group must wait for the next allowance—an inconvenience which they did not readily tolerate—and on his part the treasurer put pressure on the group to avoid waste. I remember hearing the treasurer of the Elevens warning, "We can't buy any more pencils this week if we want to go on that trip!" Once the teachers mentioned that the children were extravagant with paper towels. The towels were put in the store, to be bought instead of being supplied by the school. The wastefulness ended at once.

The store had great allure for new children, and all too quickly, too, it revealed shortcomings. One boy came to us from public school all but letter-perfect in his addition and his multiplication tables, boastful of his prowess in long division and in general pretty contemptuous of our modest level of achievement. But when he got his turn as cashier, he went completely to pieces on the task of balancing his books. He knew *how* to add, *how* to subtract—but *when* was another matter. In totaling the sales for the day he was quite as likely to subtract a sum as to add it. He had been taught the processes, and they had remained mere processes. He had a mind, however, and soon learned to use it, quite humbled when he took his lessons from one of his co-workers on whom he had previously looked down.

This was not an unusual case, but only the first of many. I do not claim that there are not ways of teaching under the traditional system which would include thinking along with rote memory. I know only that children *cannot escape* practical arithmetic if it is taught in connection with a job.

Thus our first group job came into being, and proved an overwhelming success. The children's satisfaction with it left no room for doubt. It carried them, moreover, under their teacher's skillful guidance, far afield into new learning when they began to trace the origins of some of the supplies they were handling. Paper, such an important part of their stock, led them to visit a paper mill, where they saw the process from pulp to finished product coming off the rollers. The mill foreman told them, when they asked, that the pulp had been made from trees in the Adirondacks and Canada. Back at school they traced on maps the route the pulp might take by boat or train, and listened to stories of lumberjacks read aloud. They wrote their own lumber camp stories and acted them out in the classroom and in rhythms period. In science they tried their hands at papermaking from rags and from wood pulp, and acquired a wholesome respect for the industrialized process.

They experimented with paints and dyes. They wrote letters to pencil factories asking permission to visit, and were disappointed and at the same time curious when permission was refused because of trade secrets, a mysterious phrase into which they immediately inquired. The manufacturers did send them samples of pencils in various stages of manufacture, and leaflets telling about the graphite mines on Lake Champlain and the Florida cedar wood. Maps were again consulted; some of the children made what they called "pencil maps," showing the sources of materials and the routes by which they were brought to the factories.

The rubber used for the erasers led them to a steamer just in from the Amazon with a cargo of crude rubber hams. Hills of Brazil nuts piled on the dock, sailors with pet monkeys— they raced back to school with their noses full of the pungent aroma of the tropics, and hunted out in books and on maps everything they could find about the Amazon valley. The classroom blossomed with gorgeously imaginative paintings of the jungle and the native rubber gatherers. I challenge anyone to suggest a more glamorous way to learn geography, short of traveling around the world in person—and I wish we could do that with the children too!

They followed lines of inquiry back into the past as well as out into space, historical as well as geographical lines. Their store led them to ask about earlier kinds of stores, about the first ones set up on Manhattan Island; they looked into barter among the Indians and fur-trading posts. They read for themselves stories of the first settlers, of the Dutch on Manhattan Island; the more difficult original accounts by explorers were read aloud by the teacher. They found fascinating the minute details, the cumulative masses of trivia so important in a picture of a strange way of life, with which the pioneers interlarded their diaries and narratives of travels on land and sea. They inquired constantly into the relationships between the white men and the Indians. And again they got out their maps, to follow the trails of the fur traders and compare them with the routes of modern railways, and note the physical features of the land, the rivers and mountains which determined the way a man would take on his journey. They speculated on the relative advantages enjoyed by the Dutch traders along the Hudson, the French on the St. Lawrence, the English in New England, and they backed up their opinions by the map.

Early in the year, when the setting up of the store was so absorbing a task, I had worried about the children. Please, I begged Nell Moore, don't let them become tired businessmen at the age of eight! Make them play a little, too!

But I needn't have worried. The children found their own balance between work and play. They were constantly making believe, both indoors and out. An icy day in the yard was just the day for lumberjacks; or else they borrowed the large yard blocks of the younger groups to set up trading posts and Indian shelters. Indoors they often wore costumes of their own design the whole afternoon, playing at being Dutch families in New Amsterdam. Sometimes the tales of the Mohawk valley brought back by a fur-trading father would inspire the family to move on; they played out the journey and the "making" of new land in the wilderness. A wealth of stories read aloud gave them background. They painted, modeled, danced, and sang the expression of all this new information and their ideas about it. A picture of the almost incredibly varied life of the Eights is this account, compiled from *Eight Year Old Merchants* * by Leila V. Stott:

* Copyright, 1928, Greenberg, Publisher.

A DAY WITH THE EIGHTS

"The opening discussion was on building up the map of New York State to show early trade routes of the Indians and pioneers and also the various places visited by the different children in the summer. Starting from Manhattan Island which had been drawn roughly on the blackboard, Louise showed the direction in which Henry Hudson had sailed up the river and added the Catskill Mountains where she had spent the summer. Richard put in the Palisades. Albany was located near the head of navigation and we saw how the river branched off beyond that point. Estelle had been near Schenectady in the Mohawk Valley and wanted that located so I helped her draw in the Mohawk River. Leonard added Lakes Erie and Ontario which he knew from summer experience and was helped to draw in the St. Lawrence as their outlet. Ethel had been at Lake Champlain, so with help she added that to our map. Then Edward wanted to know how to get to his home at Stockbridge and the discussion that followed added the Connecticut River and the Berkshire Mountains. Leonard said that he went through the Delaware Water Gap in traveling West, so we added the Delaware River. Further discussion added Cape Cod and Boston, and we decided to let the map stay on the board for a day or two to aid in following stories of early settlers and Indians which we are reading from the Scribner *Narratives of New Netherlands*.

"The next half hour from 9:30 to 10 was spent in practice on numbers for store work. Most of the children still need drill on addition combinations, so we played 'Mushpot' for 10 minutes and they all enjoyed this game which is conducive to speed. The rest of the time was spent on written practice in subtraction with borrowing, needed for book balancing. Those who wanted help in bookkeeping gathered at the board and papers were given out for those who preferred to work independently. Ellen, Estelle, Carl, Frank, Leonard, Ethel, and Betty came up for bookkeeping help, but Carl and Ethel were so far ahead of the rest that they had to be given harder examples to work on together.

"At 10 o'clock the group broke up for work on individual jobs. Leonard, who was store cashier for the week, had let his sales slips accumulate by skipping entries for several days and was worried about being ready for tomorrow's book balancing.

'What will happen if I don't get it done?' he asked anxiously. He was not encouraged to contemplate such an emergency and he did succeed in being ready. Ethel, as treasurer for the week, paid bills by making out checks on the teacher's bank account, in exchange for the cash from the store funds. She addressed and stamped the envelopes and took them out to mail. Carl had written an order for some new store supplies and found that his order had arrived, with a wealth of advertising material which proved so interesting that Nancy, Frank, and Richard joined him in looking it over, and Nancy wrote an order for more supplies. Frank and Richard, when they finished with the circulars, went to work on individual maps similar to the one we had put on the board. They corrected details by consulting various timetable maps and put in their relief features in plastiline. Paul worked on a new copy of the price list for the school office and Estelle, Ellen, and Edward combined on another copy asked for by Group VII. Ruth noticed that she was next on the list to be cashier and went to the teacher to say that she could never make change quickly enough for that job; she was given some special practice with real money to increase her confidence. Irene, who had never been in New York before this year, worked on a map of Manhattan to help out her local orientation. Betty and Louise drew or painted. Betty has become greatly interested in trying portrait sketches of the other children, and caught a rear view of Paul which was so characteristic that she is stimulated to further efforts. Louise seems especially interested in the use of vivid colors. Her pictures nearly always have a many-colored sunset sky or brilliantly colored house-tops grouped in effective design. She is especially strong on design and this was recognized by other children who commented on her painting as exactly suited to the paper she used. This reflected a standard that has been brought out in some recent group discussions of paintings.

"As this was a Rhythms day, all went to the gymnasium at 10:30 instead of to yard. The period began with free interpretation of music in individual pantomimes. Louise, Estelle, and Edward are always the most successful at following the pattern of the music with their feet while they carry out a dramatic idea at the same time, but today Ethel accomplished this too. Estelle started turning backward somersaults to music and Paul followed suit, making the turn without help for the first time. Louise introduced a somersault and Frank a cartwheel without losing the beat of the music. Richard proved so good at somersaults over the back of another child that Paul suggested, 'We should sell him in the store for a rubber ball.' Ruth, Ellen, and Irene, all comparatively inexperienced in Rhythms exercises, worked hard at learning to vault over wooden blocks and improved very much, though they could not keep up with the rest in that or in playing leapfrog. Miss Doing gave them special help in stretching and relaxing exercises.

"Then came the eagerly anticipated time to develop plays planned in advance by the children. For these Miss Doing furnished the kind of music asked for, 'creepy music,' 'wild music,' etc. Today Ruth organized a pantomime which she called 'The World.' Her group danced with scarves to represent fire, water, grass, sun, and wind. The original group included five of the girls plus Richard and Paul and the play was one which they had already tried spontaneously in the yard one day. Edward joined them playing 'water' to Louise's 'fire,' and these two danced a really beautiful pantomime, using colored scarves to aid in the interpretation. Miss Doing used this lead to give the whole group a chance to practice movements with the scarves to represent wind.

"The period was over all too soon and we had to hurry back to our room for the opening of the store at 11:15. Leonard, Edward, and Estelle were the store committee for the day, but Estelle was anxious to finish her part of the price list for the Sevens and asked if it would be all right to let Ruth take her place. Ruth had missed her own turn the week before through absence and needed the store work badly so this was arranged.

"At the teacher's suggestion, Edward spent his free moments between customers in studying the price list, which is hard for him to read but sufficiently interesting to be worth the effort. He would read the list of articles and examine the other two children on the prices. The student teacher went into the store with them to help in case of need so the teacher could be free to help the poorer readers. Store time is reserved as a reading period for those not on the committee. The independent readers, all but Edward, Ruth, Ellen, Nancy, and Frank, either go to the library to read or read quietly in the room, so today there were only three who needed help. Nancy had finished *Mewanee* and wanted another book as good! It was the first story she had read by herself with pleasure and she passed it on to Ellen. Nancy was given one of the Dopp series of primitive life readers and she and Ellen both read by themselves with only occasional help on hard words. Frank is a harder problem, for he is bored by the content of books easy enough for him to read alone, so the teacher read with him some historical stories and supplied words rapidly when he got stuck, so as to keep up his interest. She tried to include some incidental practice in phonetics to help in discovering new words, but had to be careful not to overdo it or his interest in the story would be lost.

"The others read peacefully until they were called to wash for lunch. They seemed to enjoy the relaxation after the strenuous exercise in Rhythms. As they finished washing, those who wanted appointments for the afternoon in shop, laboratory, or clay modeling studio brought their cards to be signed.

"After lunch all had a half hour of rest stretched out on mats in the gymnasium and came back at one o'clock ready for an hour of outdoor play.

"It was a beautiful fall day and the teacher wanted to encourage more free dramatic play in the yard as she felt they had had too much of organized games. She again offered them some costumes to use in outdoor play as they had done the previous month and it was suggested they use the younger children's yard, which was free at this time and was equipped with large blocks for dramatic play. All but Ethel and Richard entered into the idea with interest. Leonard, Frank, and Edward set up a wigwam as they had done last month. Nancy and Carl organized a trading post and there was loosely organized trading play between the two groups with the rest of the children joining one or the other. When some of the boys began to lose interest and become silly, the teacher suggested that they watch each other's plays. This resulted in two definite scenes played with greatly increased organization and interest. The first was an Indian scene in which Ellen and Betty were squaws, chiefly occupied in tending the fire, while Frank and Edward were braves who went hunting with imaginary bows and arrows. They brought in boards to represent deer, skinned them and tanned the skins (still using the boards), which they took to Nancy and Louise at the trading store; gave the venison (more boards) to the squaws to cook;

and made tom-toms out of stretched pieces of skin; ending their scene by beating with sticks upon the same boards which now represented the finished tom-toms.

"The second story, played by Frank, Leonard, Edward, and Carl, was a representation of Adrian Block's adventures in Manhattan from the loss by fire of his trading post to the building of the first white man's house on the island. Finally, they extended the scene to the building of a ship, in which the party departed for home after realistic raising of the anchor and hoisting of the sails.

"The next hour from two to three was the time reserved for individual appointments in the school shops or other individual work in the classroom. Richard and Ethel as usual went to the clay room. They have become very friendly through a common interest in this work and the sociability of the clay room is helping Ethel more than anything else to feel at home in the school. They are now glazing their products to be fired in the school kiln for Christmas presents.

"Carl, Ruth, Betty, Estelle, and Leonard went to the laboratory as a committee who have volunteered to do some special research for the group on primitive industries of pioneer days. The first three are making candles and soap and the last two, dugouts. Frank as usual had a card for shop, made out till 3:30, the longest possible period (one hour and a half), and another for an after-school appointment. He is making window boxes for his mother and is insistent on finding time to finish them. In view of the fact that he had been reported as lacking in concentration when he first came into the school a year ago, this tendency to work in long periods interests me particularly. I have not observed lack of concentration in any other school activity either, except in reading.

"Irene and Louise had appointments for individual work in music, for which there is great demand by all the children. Miss Hubbell has a little free time and reserves half an hour once a week for the Eights besides their two regular group lessons. Today Louise wanted to compose some music to the words of a song she has written, but she first joined Irene in making musical patterns on the tone bars, practicing on the drum and bouncing balls to changing meters. In the last seven minutes of the period she produced her original song, 'good in form and interesting in spirit and rhythm,' according to Miss Hubbell's report. Irene contributed a good phrase of her own to the song and made clever comments on Louise's phrases.

"The other children, Edward, Nancy, Paul, and Ellen, stayed in the classroom to paint. Paul is now well launched in enjoyment of color and design and in self-confidence. He still mixes all his colors with infinite pains and paints abstract designs only. He evidently has a story in his own mind, for today he showed a finished design with the comment, 'Down here where you see these checked figures is the family and the lines going round are soldiers protecting them from the enemy.' He still has an unfinished bird house in the shop but it is so good to have him interested in more imaginative lines that I have not reminded him of the bird house. There is no danger of irresponsibility with him.

"Ellen is still painting the kind of picture that has grass below and sky above and houses and trees in a straight line, and I am trying to get her interested in Paul's kind of abstract design for a change. No luck so far.

"Nancy and Edward worked near together as they often do, talking over their paintings, criticizing and suggesting to one another. They planned together a series of pictures, done on a large scale, called Pig and Co. The first picture, done by Nancy, shows a truck dumping pigs into the water to be drowned; the next, done by Edward, shows another truck carrying the drowned pigs to the butcher. Many of the details in both pictures reflect actual experience of street scenes freely adapted to the story. Nancy is adding a third picture, showing the farmer starting the pigs on their fatal journey. Both children know that drowning is not the approved method of slaughtering pigs, but they seem to prefer it as less brutal.

"By three o'clock most of the group had gathered for our final half hour of reading aloud. We are still reading *Rolf in the Woods*, a story by Thompson-Seton which deals with adventures of colonial days, canoeing, fur trapping, and trading in the territory between the Hudson and Connecticut rivers, so the content fits in well with our present interests. We used the map we had put on the board this morning to follow the story, and several children contributed individual maps of their own showing the same territory. Frank stayed in the shop and Richard in the clay room, but Ethel, much as she loves the clay work, was back promptly so as not to miss the story. I never insist that the children come back for it, but even if they skip the reading occasionally, they manage to keep track of the story well enough to follow it with real enjoyment. Only Edward never joins the group for reading but draws or paints quietly in the back of the room. I try to read softly enough to exclude him, as I want to encourage concentration both in listening to a story and in painting, but Edward's successful share yesterday in dramatic representation of a part of the story would indicate that he has taken in more of it than might have been expected.

"There was great competition as usual to have the seat next to the teacher during the reading, until Leonard announced he was holding the seat for Paul, since he is deaf in one ear and 'ought to have it.' Paul had it by common consent!"

CHAPTER NINE

MORE JOBS
FOR CHILDREN

ONCE THE eight-year-olds had proved the value of jobs—had proved not only that children could and would carry on a serious enterprise over as long a period as an entire school year, but, further, that the job was a natural steppingstone to learning of all kinds, even, indeed most particularly, to the three R's—it was inevitable that an idea with such vitality should spread throughout the upper school. The question was no longer whether there should be jobs for children, but what the jobs should be.

We turned for the answer, as always, to the children. The Eights, meanwhile, were asking a few questions of their own. It was spring, and they were thinking ahead to the next year when they would be Nines. What, they wanted to know, was going to happen to their store? Could they take it with them?

Their teacher suggested that they could offer it to one of the older groups (we had children of nine and ten in the school by then) or to the oncoming class. As to the older groups, said these Eights, nothing doing. The new Eights, however, were another matter. It was only fair to give them the store, if they wanted it.

The new Eights did want it, and most positively, despite dire warnings concerning hard work, the business of keeping accounts, the amount of arithmetic they would have to learn. And now the little storekeepers became pressing; the old Nines might have been willing to do without a job, but not they. What was their next job to be?

Nell Moore had a proposal: the store experience had shown the need for mail orders; also the telephone calls to classrooms were a problem. A school post office could be a real service. And so the pioneers, as they began now to call themselves, started a school post office.

For ideas on equipment they visited a branch post office, and soon they were measuring off a corner of their new classroom, toiling in the shop over shelves, a counter, pigeonholes, and cash boxes, and turning out a mail box for each floor. They experimented with ways of making stamped envelopes to be sold for mail within the school: linoleum cuts mounted on a handle, one for first-class and another for second-class mail, were the result. They set up a schedule of mail collections and deliveries every hour, and opened the post office to the school for a half hour daily to sell supplies.

Over a period of years, group after group of ambitious entrepreneurs added new features to the post office. They began to sell United States postage stamps, postal cards, and stamped envelopes as a convenience to teachers, parents, and the school office. They inaugurated a Special Delivery service for urgent messages. Finally, and most ambitious of all, they instituted a Parcel Post service. Begun at the request of the office, which was handling orders for our published school records, this Parcel Post service found itself really in demand when the parents got wind of it and began to use it for their Christmas packages. A real "busy season" developed in December, which gave these youngsters a job big enough even for their insatiable appetite. They weighed the packages, looked up the rates on a regular Postal Zone chart secured from the local branch, figured the postage, stamped the packages, and carried them to the branch for mailing. It was exercise in more than merely the muscular sense; they learned a good deal about their own country, its cities and states, while their multiplication tables had a very thorough going over when postage was being figured.

As they had visited grown-up stores to learn about storekeeping, now they visited post offices, not only the local branch, but railway mail cars, steamer pier post offices, and the impressive Main Post Office of New York City.

The smaller branches, like that at the Lackawanna Station in Hoboken, were wonderful, for there the men were not too busy. They allowed the children actually to help sort letters into the proper pigeonholes. The children lost not a moment, back at school, in providing their own Postmaster with stamp and ink pad for canceling letters—with dates—in the school mail.

The Main Post Office was a big and serious adventure. Their letter to the Postmaster of New York City, asking permission to visit, had brought a reply granting their request on condition that they would come first to his office for an interview. This busy and important official took time to discuss their school post office with them, and then proceeded to enlist them all as Post Office Helpers. He showed them how stamps placed in the wrong corner, incomplete or illegible addresses, and other such carelessness interfered with the efficiency of the mail service, and made them promise to help spread knowledge of the right way to address and stamp a letter. He gave them a collection of stories to take back to school—a history of the United States Post Office, true adventures in the delivery of mail on the Pacific Coast, the Great Lakes, and in far-off snowy Alaska. And he ended by presenting them with a copy of the heroic Post Office motto, the very one carved across the front of the massive building in which they stood—"Neither rain nor snow . . . shall stay these couriers . . ."—to hang in their own little post office. They wore solemn little faces indeed when they came back to school that day.

But not too solemn for several of them to make tracks for the science room, where they demanded more information on the pneumatic tube system by which mail was distributed from the Main Post Office to branches throughout the city, and an experiment to show them how air pressure worked.

The Postmaster would have been pleased to know that although the reading matter he gave them was too difficult for most of them to read, in small typewriter type, it was thoroughly used. The teacher read it aloud to them, then at their request rewrote it into simpler form and had it typed in the office in large type for them to read by themselves. Some of the stories finally emerged in dramatic dialogue which they delighted to use for practice in reading aloud.

There were other stories to read and listen to, stories of the Pony Express, of the mail coaches, travelers' own accounts full of the detail which had pleased the children so much in their reading of pioneer stories the year before. Taking its departure from the mail service, their history and geography broadened to embrace the westward movement and the building of railroad and telegraph lines across the continent. Airmail service brought them back again to the present—not without some speculation even into the future— and the high point of the year was the trip to the airport for their final spring picnic.

In time, as the school grew larger, the teachers felt the store was a little too much for eight-year-olds, and the Eights and Nines switched jobs. The Eights, running the post office, were not likely to go quite so far afield in their investigations; they stayed closer to home, studying the Post Roads to Albany, Boston, Philadelphia, the settlers along them and their ways of living. The Nines used the store as a jumping-off point for a study of trade routes like the Santa Fe trail and the westward movement of settlers who followed them, the sources of materials, the geographical conditions which produced them—trade is a never-ending thread to pursue. Their laboratory experiments dealt with the making of paper, soap, candles as the early settlers had made them; with electricity as in the telegraph and telephone, with steam in the working of steam engines. So rich have been the opportunities for investigation opened by the store, in fact, that different groups of Nines through the years have found different fields beckoning. Sometimes it has been the pioneers in their covered wagons opening the way to the westward, sometimes the clipper ship captains who rounded the Horn to China.

The fact that the actual subject matter which dominated the Nines' program—or any other group's program—has not been identical from one year to the next has never disturbed us. What was important was not so much *what* the children studied, but that they learned *how* to study: how to gather their facts at first hand and from every source they could find; how to understand what they were learning, relate it, make it their own in picture and story and song and play; absorb it so well, under the impetus of their own interest and desire to learn, that it would be theirs forever.

For the ten-year-olds we had tried printing with a hand press, for there was a real need for printing to be met. The Sevens wanted copies of their City News about the events in their play city; for the moment, these copies which became their actual reading matter were being run off on a large-type typewriter in the office.

But the Tens, as we found, were not quite ready to be printers—the technique was too difficult for them. The Sevens' teacher had another job for them, however, which was equally urgent and needful. She was swamped by the multitude of reading charts, flash cards, and sentence strips she was hand-lettering as drill material for the beginning readers. She would be delighted to give the Tens regular orders for these to be done in their best manuscript writing. It was not an easy job, involving as it did a good deal of careful measuring as well as nearly perfect lettering. But the Tens, flattered by the prospect of having their writing used as a model by the younger children, and of being really helpful to a teacher in her work, eagerly took it on. It is a happy thing to see how sympathetically the children have responded to any request for help for those younger than themselves, just such willing and thoughtful cooperation as we have found grownups eager to give the children on their trips in search of information. As the Eights had pointed out the fairness of handing their beloved store over to the group which came after them, so the Tens were now willing to undertake a tough assignment on behalf of the Sevens.

Their teacher was happy with the new job, too. She saw an opportunity for needed work in improving their handwriting and for learning to use ink. The measuring and spacing, the setting of prices on their work, would offer good arithmetic experience in addition to their bookkeeping, and would lead them quite naturally into work with fractions. Beyond the skills, an interest in writing and records would open up a rich field of the far-away and long-ago for which these children were plainly ready. On trips to the museum they were forever wandering into the Egyptian rooms or the Mediaeval armor collection; in the school library they were seeking out romantic stories of the Age of Chivalry. The project promised well, and the Tens embarked on it with a large back log of orders.

The whole group began with writing practice in ink. As soon as any child felt ready to begin on an order, he chose his job from those available and was shown how to rule a strip of tag board according to specifications and measure out his letter spaces. An order was completed at the child's own speed. Originally the teacher passed on the work, but presently the class business manager objected that the teacher's standard was too low! Thereafter teacher and children jointly decided whether the work was satisfactory.

Setting prices for the work was a real life arithmetic problem. Each child wrote a sample card with the same number of letters and measured the time it took him. Then the group figured the average speed—so many letters per hour—and prices were set per number of letters at the accepted school rate of fifteen cents an hour. Thus each worker could go at his own pace, without the necessity of watching his time. The time spent daily on the job varied according to orders, but no child ever spent more than an hour in any one day on writing, seldom more than forty minutes, and there were many days with no jobs at all. These days the children worked on fine mansucript writing and illuminating. They looked upon this exercise, which they loved, as part of their job.

Still the Tens' opportunities for making money were limited compared with the other groups. This was important, a tangible measure of the value of the service performed and the seriousness of the enterprise in adult eyes. We had established from the first, in setting up the store with the Eights, the principle that the children were performing a service for the school and should be paid regular wages. At the rate of fifteen cents an hour, the storekeepers and postal workers received fifteen cents each at the end of each month, on the rough calculation that each child spent an hour on store or post office work in the course of the month. And the satisfaction of taking home that pay envelope each month never palled, any more than an adult's satisfaction in collecting his own salary!

The Tens, on the other hand, were paid piece-work wages as a group, and divided the income. When they found their venture was not as profitable as they desired, they began to take orders for Christmas cards, decorating them with linoleum cuts of their own making. They worked as a group on an order, with a business manager to take the order and assign the work, and a business treasurer to collect for the finished orders and keep the accounts.

These class offices and any others, as with the jobs in the store and the post office, were passed around the group in rotation, each child serving for a week at a time and all having a fair share of the work. When the teacher suggested that perhaps a certain child was not ready to undertake a certain job, the unanswerable question came from the group, "How can he learn if he never gets a chance to try?"

While the writing job has held the interest of the Tens and met school needs well enough to last for more than a decade, our teachers from time to time have criticized it, principally because it did not provide enough physical activity and practical responsibility. To fill the gap, the Tens presently undertook a second job, that of the lunchroom. They provided a squad of waiters to set the tables, clear them, and refill dishes for second helpings on demand, and the rotating job of head-waiter came to carry a good deal of prestige. Their interest in food became keen enough for them to request special cooking appointments, and to prepare on occasion some dish of their choice for the school lunch. They undertook to check the monthly food bills, and once reaped the glorious reward of discovering an overcharge of two dollars on a milk bill. "It's worth while to do all that arithmetic when you can find two dollars," was the sage comment of the child who made the official report to the school treasurer.

The lettering project meanwhile continued to expand in a way most gratifying to the Tens. New requests sprang up— for door cards to go on the classroom doors, bearing the group number in Roman numerals and the teacher's name; for menu cards to be posted in the luncheon; for large charts with the words of songs to go on the music room wall. These last gave the Tens a chance to let themselves go in a riot of marginal illustrations and illuminated capitals. "Of course we can't charge for the decorations," they explained reasonably, "we just put them in for pleasure."

The inspiration for this kind of pleasure came from trips to see the beautifully illuminated old manuscripts in the Morgan Library and the main Public Library. Sometimes I have wondered whether it is not the children's interest in the information to which their writing leads them which has kept alive their enthusiasm for their group job. While they practiced the forms of fine lettering they discussed the origins of writing, from the familiar picture writing of our own Indians through the hieroglyphics of Egypt to the first real alphabets of the Semitic peoples. Cards appeared like a frieze around the walls of their room, bearing the alphabets of the Phoenicians, the Hebrews, the Greeks, the Romans (which the children were astonished to find was their own, with a few letters missing), while the children followed the trail of writing around the shores of the Mediterranean and studied the life of this cradle of Western civilization.

They were quick to compare this new knowledge with what they already knew of our pioneer civilization at home. I remember once that the group was listening to a story of the Phoenicians, in which it was mentioned that piracy was considered by them to be the worst crime. "Naturally that would be so, with sea people," came the comment, "just as cattle-stealing was the worst crime for our western cowboys." This was the kind of thinking for which we worked consciously from pre-school years on, this thinking in terms of general principles which comes from the habit of recognizing relationships between one bit of information and the next, and it was a satisfaction when we found such clear evidence that it was taking root.

From the ancient civilizations the group progressed to the Middle Ages, and promptly fell in love with its romantic trappings, painting heraldic devices on their windows, and playing knights and ladies with such gusto that their teacher eventually had to remind them there were other kinds of people living in those days, people whose lives were far less glamorous. Their investigation into the way the work of the feudal world was done, and by whom, enlisted their ready sympathy for the serfs, and before long they were with equal gusto tracing the growth of democratic ideas down to the present.

The Elevens fell heir to the printing job which we had tried with the Tens and postponed. With a year more of growth, we found, they were ready and able to take over this very complex and exacting work, most of them with such enthusiasm, in fact, that it was difficult to wean them away from it at the end of the year. When we added an electric press to the original foot press, some groups tried to carry printing into their next year's work, but this made for confusion, and children and teachers agreed in the end to leave printing entirely to the Elevens.

The Elevens came to be the busiest and the highest-income group in the school. In addition to printing the Sevens' reading material, the need which created the print shop, they undertook to do all the job printing for the school—attendance lists, library cards—and later for the Parents' Association as well, such as stationery and the heading on the parents' mimeographed news sheet. At the end of the year they produced their masterpiece, a magazine of stories and poems, their own or chosen from the whole school, with linoleum cuts or wood cuts made by themselves for illustration.

Our first group of printers organized themselves as craftsmen did in the old guilds, setting up a series of tests for apprentices, journeymen, and master printers; the tests vary from year to year in some small detail, but the system has become a tradition in the school. Make-ready and lock-up and the mysteries of the California job case were the shop talk of the Elevens. At the end of the year, with a good deal of ceremony, certificates were presented to the journeymen and master printers—certificates ordered from the Tens and executed on fine parchment paper with the Tens' handsomest manuscript writing and most lavish illuminations.

Printing led them in natural progression from the Mediaeval interests of their previous year into the invention of printing and the flowering of the Renaissance, a chronological sequence binding these two years together which the children recognized delightedly. The Crusades, the story of Marco Polo, and the opening of trade with China carried their geography as well as their history around the world. Their arithmetic grew more precise, with multiplication and division of fractions to enable them to lay out their type on a page, and with quite complicated figuring of costs of materials and especially of labor in the billing of their clients, since apprentices received five cents an hour, journeymen ten cents, and master printers fifteen cents. While the Tens dealt with language in fairly simple forms, the Elevens in their printing found their acquaintance with the more advanced mechanics of English growing rapidly, with a marked emphasis on the literary side.

My first suggestion for a job for the Twelves had been toy-making, in particular the small wooden dolls, the "little people" and animals which the younger children needed in block-building. The toys which had been in use ever since the school started were by now pretty well exhausted and even rather out of date. The Twelves promptly organized the "Never Bust Toy Company" and turned out dolls and animals of their own design. They submitted them for criticism to me and to the Sixes and Sevens who would use them, and then manufactured them as ordered, with the girls making rather a specialty of painting on the costumes for engineers, street cleaners, farmers, ship captains, women and children, and the horses, cows, sheep, pigs, and chickens. They made automobiles and boats as well, not for the little children, who preferred to make their own, but for sale to parents for the children to use in their block play at home. After the Christmas sale which introduced the toy company to parents, they were fairly swamped with orders, and the Twelves were so pleased with their job that when we decided to keep them for another year as the school's first group of Thirteens, they continued the toy company for at least part of that year.

A group of literary Twelves came some years later, after toy-making had given place to weaving for a few years. These youngsters relegated the toy-making for the younger children to a voluntary basis for the manual-minded, and set out on an entirely original enterprise, that of a monthly publication, *The Bookworm's Digest*. In it they reviewed new children's books sent them at their request by the publishers, and added a column called Old Favorites, especially to pass on to the younger children their experience with what the school library had to offer. The younger children, it should be said, generally gave this advice their respectful attention, and since the publishers found the publication worthy of attention and the library welcomed the many valuable additions among the book review copies, the enterprise as a whole was a fine success.

With such a job as this came a welcome emphasis on written English work, embracing the mechanics of grammar and spelling as well as more literary aspects. We introduced a special course called Word Study, an introduction to the history of words and the structure of the English language. Our intention was to arouse more interest and understanding for the troublesome problem of spelling, but as always happened when a project enlisted the children's own urge to learn, the subject carried them further than we in our planning had dared anticipate. The roots from Latin and Greek, the literal meanings of words and their transformations through the centuries, the building of words by prefixes and suffixes caught the children's imagination, and our graduates have come back to report a lively gratitude for the help this study had given them in an understanding of language, especially in beginning foreign languages.

Perhaps because they were by now reading the daily newspapers with ease, the Twelves showed a sharp awareness of contemporary events, and, with the flexibility of a teaching approach which is tuned to the children's own interests, we quickly took advantage of this. We found that a coal strike, a crisis in Latin-American relations, or almost any substantial situation which occupied the headlines of the day, was as good a place to begin the Twelves' informational program as any. Sooner or later their quest for the sources of today's social and economic problems led them back to the industrial revolution where such problems generally have their beginnings, and around again in a full circle to the present-day scene.

In their thirteenth year the children themselves accepted the responsibilities of this last year before high school. They took stock of their academic achievement and concentrated on polishing up where it was needed. Very often, too, they have looked back on the school they were soon to leave, and affectionately set their hand to some permanent improvement they might leave behind them. One group transformed the lunchroom annex with a complete paint job, new tables made and decorated by themselves, and new curtains for the windows. During the war years they constituted themselves the handymen of the school, doing all sorts of repairs for which carpenters, painters, and electricians were not to be had. The responsible jobs which thirteen-year-olds could execute with skill were a constant astonishment to their parents, and occasionally even to us who knew their accomplishments so well.

If any one enterprise can be said to have dominated the Thirteens' year, it has been photography. A frequent out-of-school hobby among children of this age, with us it marched right into the school and became both a school service—a photographic record enhanced the school's file on individual children—and a spur to eager activity in the science room. In about thirty hours' work through the year each child had acquired the technique of developing, enlarging and printing, and completed his share of the job. Many simple experiments in physics and chemistry grew out of the practical experience in the dark room.

Along with a chronological study of American history, the Thirteens continued to reach out from current events toward causes and effects. The mushrooming growth of industry in their own country interested them and led them along new trails and on numerous trips. The impact of mass production —as in a visit to a Ford assembly plant—had a curious effect on these individual little workers accustomed to develop at their leisure an artistic product.

Not only the Thirteens, but some of the younger children,

were inspired to comment on this kind of experience. Here is
a description by a boy of eleven, of the press room of a great
daily newspaper:

> Intricate and immense the great press stands
> And the roar of it is like a dull background
> Against which the brilliant little noises
> Weave a pattern of sound.

From the Thirteens came the following, the first after the
trip to the Ford plant, the second inspired by a mass meeting
in Union Square:

Machines

> The motor, the body, and then the wheel
> Are put on by men who do not feel.
> They stand at their jobs from twelve to ten;
> They are grimy, oily, mechanical men.
>
> Some turn a screw, some paint it tan,
> Each part done by the one same man.
> The chain of cars rolls on its way—
> They are cars that are made in half a day.
>
> Who makes these cars of nickel and steel?
> Who puts them together with speed unreal?
> Just men—men earning their living,
> Really not taking, only giving.
>
> For as they work there day after day
> Their minds grow stupid, their brains decay.
> They are now only grimy mechanical men,
> Yes, just grimy, oily, mechanical men.

The Orator

> He stands aloft the crowd,
> And shouts and bites.
> His harsh voice cuts the air,
> He shouts out in defiance.
> The mob nods its head,
> The orator sweats.
> He's a mess, he must be crazy!
> Is he?

One hour, two hours, his arms wave wildly,
His eyes glare.
The mob moves slowly, slowly off.
He *must* be crazy!
Is he?

The post office, the store, the print shop, the photography studio, so satisfying to our children, are not the inevitable answer for children in a different environment. A country school might find, for instance, that a chicken industry was better for eight- or nine-year-olds, while an older group could make a very worth-while experience out of running a cooperative store on a larger scale than our Nines' stationery store.

In a big public-school system like that of New York City, on the other hand, where supplies for all the schools are centrally ordered, a store with buying and selling for cash is impossible. Even here, however, a group of children may operate a distributing center for supplies. Such a plan has been tried successfully, and several other original enterprises as well. I am proud that one of our former teachers, Adele Franklin, was the moving spirit in bringing into being such enterprises in a big public school.

Jobs as the core of an elementary-school curriculum have proved themselves to our satisfaction over and over again, and from every point of view. The absorption of the children in their jobs, the way in which, like healthy plants, they throw roots out in every direction from the job to draw in ever more educational nourishment—in the practical skills, in geography and history, in literature and music and the arts—to us this is the surest confirmation that we have enlisted that potent and precious force, the child's urge to learn, in his education.

To the stern eye of the traditional educator, who might discount the child's satisfaction in his job as of little more importance than the sugar coating on a pill, the school's primary purpose, beyond teaching children to read, write, and

Study leads to art…

...and rhythms.

reckon, is the building of character. This excellent standard for an educational philosophy is the one most frequently saluted by school authorities. I have always wondered what part of the traditional system is counted on to do the character-building. Is it the discipline of learning lessons whose purpose—to the child—is mysterious and whose content is only accidentally interesting?

I watched with satisfaction the conversion to the job idea of one of our teachers. She went so far as to accept "activities" in a school program, but side-stepped jobs. After she had become principal of her own school she came back to me with a question which troubled her: why were the children of the City and Country School so much more responsible in their work than the children of her own school?

It was my opportunity. I looked her in the eye and said only the word, "Jobs!" She had to admit, in the good-natured laughter which followed, that the children had proved my point.

CHAPTER TEN

BOOK-LEARNING
HAS ITS TURN

IF THE anxious father, who wondered whether we were preparing his son for Harvard, has come this far with me, he may still be asking the same question and with the same anxiety. "All right, all right, you've been talking about *how* the children learn," he may say rather testily (as often enough he has), "but you haven't told me *what* they learn. What's going to happen to my boy when he comes face to face with trigonometry?"

I could tell him about the twelve-year-old lad who learned long division by way of cosines and cotangents—he had a

scientific bent, and took a notion to study navigation by tri-
angulation, and since he needed to learn his long division we
had no objection to the round-about way he took to learn it.
I could tell him about the ten-year-old who found out how
to figure the cubic contents of a vessel, and the ones who
measured the heights of buildings by angles—but it wouldn't
be quite fair, since these have been rather special instances
even for us, who know that the average child is a figment of
the statistician's imagination and don't expect ever to meet
such a child in real life.

I must admit that a traditional school's curriculum is much
more reassuring to such a father, or to the mother who demanded, "But what will become of these children—*will they
ever be bank presidents, or directors of corporations?*" The
subject matter of a traditional school is fixed and immovable:
in the third grade a child is given just so much of required history, of geography, of science, of arithmetic and reading and
writing. A glance at a chart will tell the precise contents of a
child's mind when he has finished his sixth or seventh or
eighth year of school.

Or will it? Perhaps the principals and superintendents who
laid out the system on paper believe that it will, and the
parents who keep their eyes on Harvard or bank presi-
dencies. But I have never found any such easy way to read
a child's mind. On the other hand, it was when I discovered,
in my early teaching days, that the things the curriculum
was supposed to have put into his mind really weren't there
at all, that I began to look about for some other, surer method
of getting children to learn what they must learn in order to
live competently in a complex world.

The system of pouring so much history, so much geography, so much arithmetic into a child—like a recipe for making
bread—was very fine except for one slight fault: it did not
work. Some children, like yeast, would rise anyway, no
matter how the ingredients of education were mixed. But
those children are rare, and why should they or any children
be expected to absorb stated quantities of unrelated informa-

tion at stated chronological periods? Children simply do not grow that way!

Even the strictest traditionalist is now no longer so sure that his chart of the child's learning agrees with the facts. Under the pressure of progressive education and of parents who have a truer understanding of the nature of a child, the systems are being "enriched": a little more painting, modeling, music, handicraft; the introduction of "activities," of "projects." The inertia of a huge public school system is enormous, and change is painful and slow, but the need for change is being recognized.

As for our anxious father, I could not undertake to diagram the contents of his son's mind on the day the boy leaves our hands at the age of thirteen. I could assure him, however, that if the moment of meeting trigonometry is frightening to him, it is not to the boy himself. If he has learned anything, he has learned to meet situations and cope with them. Trigonometry is one more situation to him, and he will handle it.

Yet it is true that educators have quarreled over the subject matter of schools, and we have spent many a long staff meeting on the problem. The children themselves had pointed out to us in unmistakable ways that "the proper study of mankind is man." But with the whole world to explore, there must be some principle of selection.

As the group jobs developed, we found to our gratification that they provided not only a core to which the work of each year could be related—that arithmetic and history, for example, were as much a part of the store job as selling pencils—but that they also established a kind of selectivity in the wide field of human knowledge. The eight-year-old post office workers, following the story of the Post Roads, delved into the lives of the settlers and the Indians on the one hand; on the other hand, they were investigating the nature of air pressure in the science room, because they had seen pneumatic tubes in the Main Post Office.

Indeed, so fast and so far did the children's interest in their jobs lead them, that on occasion I found it necessary to call

them back. The origin of written records among the Chinese
seemed to me too much of a good thing for ten-year-olds.
But the children themselves generally showed how far they
ought to go. They were like the small boy who asked, "How
far away is the moon?"

"Too far away for us to reach it," was the answer.

"Couldn't an airplane, a very fast one, reach it?"

"No, not even a very fast one."

"Let's talk about something else."

Just so, when a subject got too far away for them to reach
it, the children made it clear in one way or another that they
would rather talk about something else.

Thus, roughly, our subject matter came to include everything that is taught in a traditional school, besides much,
much more. What was different was our approach. Instead
of putting teacher and children into a straitjacket at the out-
set with a rigid set of requirements for the year's work, we
allowed the job, the group's interests, the events that were
the talk of the dinner table at night or the headlines of the
morning paper to guide them. Each group teacher kept in
mind the needs of the next year's job in skills, and found ways
to prepare the children for them. Staff discussions laid down
in broad outline the direction each year's work would follow
and the subject matter it was likely to cover, but each group,
as it went through the school, took its own way also through
the many fields of learning spread before it. And they
acquired, not only habits of learning that would see them
through a lifetime (through Harvard, too, and even through
a bank presidency!), but also an amazing quantity of sheer
information—absorbed it, understood it, held it ready for use
when they needed it.

The older children's progress through their subject matter
was of course more complex than that of the little ones whose
trips and discussions and learning through play dealt with
what was familiar and close to home. The use of books became an absorbing activity in its own right.

Because we had put off secondhand experience until they

had got their feel of learning at first hand about the familiar world close by, they approached their learning from books with a real appetite for knowledge of things more distant in time and space. They approached it, moreover, with very much the same method of practical scientific inquiry by which they had learned to gather information on the trips of their earlier years. Books as such, or museums or art galleries, held no terrors for them. The printed word aroused in them neither awe nor fear of boredom; children who had traveled up and down the city to learn what they wanted to know, who had found postmasters and stevedores and busy factory foremen willing to answer their questions, were not likely to be intimidated by a book. Nor did they expect to be bored in the course of learning—how could they be? They had always gone after knowledge on the momentum of their own curiosity and interest, and had developed the ability to pursue knowledge by exercising it, like a well used muscle. If one book did not give them what they sought, if it was too wordy or too hard or off the subject, they had no hesitation in putting it aside and trying another. They had had too much fun out of finding out what they wanted to know to be easily discouraged.

Obviously this kind of young researcher demands a certain kind of library, and this we had. With Margaret Ernst as librarian, our library had grown up with the school in response to the children's actual needs. Most of the books in it were there because they had been tried out by the teachers and the children. Many of them were bought only after they had been tested in actual use; in the early days we borrowed from the traveling library division of the public libraries, and bought our permanent library, book by proven book, with the comments of the children who had read them as a constant guide.

For their part the librarians developed an original system of indexing according to topic. Under the head *Printing*, for example, they would list not only the technical and historical books on printing, but also all the story books the library had which touched upon the subject. Portions of a life of Gutenberg would be read by the teacher to the whole group, but an individual eleven-year-old, spurred by a reference to the earlier invention of printing in China, might seek under the subject *Printing* for a story book on China, and find it there if it had something about printing in it.

Reading for pleasure, incidentally, received the same serious consideration from the librarians. For story books they developed their own index system out of the kind of requests that come from children, requests for "a story about a dog" or "a cowboy story" or "a story with baseball in it." In less time than one would think, these children were not asking for help but were consulting the index independently. The seven- and eight-year-olds, just taking their first steps into the world of books, had a shelf all to themselves of easy readers where they could browse and make their own choices. The older children had no trouble finding more books by an author they had enjoyed, under the author's name. They had written authors' names and the titles of books on library cards with their own hands, since the first day they had gone to the library. Index cards were no mystery to them.

The children of nine were not too young, we found, to begin doing research on a given topic in books, with a library planned for their needs and librarians ready to help them find what they wanted. A trip or a class discussion or a book read aloud by the teacher would lead to a number of questions, and the children would choose among them, each according to his own bent, the topics on which they would work. Learning to find the books they needed was only the first step in their independent research. They also had to learn to read for specific information, not merely to copy down what they found, but to select from it what was pertinent and important—in this, too, the librarians guided them.

The teachers' choice of reading matter for the classroom was submitted to constant re-examination. Diaries, letters, and firsthand narratives of the life and times which they were studying proved the most absorbing kind of reading-aloud to the children. I urged the teachers not to limit themselves to children's literature, and they roamed the whole field of books for literary treasure-trove. One teacher read parts of *Maria Chapdelaine* to her eight-year-olds, and so vivid was the picture they drew from her reading of life among the pioneers that when the children wondered in their discussions why people moved out of settled communities to live under such primitive conditions, they brought up characters in the novel as cases in point. A teacher of the Elevens read passages from Erasmus' *In Praise of Folly* with her class, and got from them a batch of entertaining little satires of their own composition, in praise of homework, mud, stopped clocks and other antic subjects. This same group dipped still further into philosophy on its own, bringing in a batch of the sayings of Confucius which the class enjoyed analyzing for their wisdom and their penetrating wit.

Far from taking the place of firsthand experience, we found that research in books was just as likely to lead these children right out of the library again, to the science room for an experiment, or on a trip to see something with their own eyes. A story of the Phoenicians plying the Mediterranean with cargoes of tin led one boy to try making bronze in our laboratory, and his report of his experiment stimulated a trip for the whole class to a modern bronze foundry.

The science room thus became for the children what a science room should be, another place where they could go to learn what they wanted to know. There was for the older children an organized body of work in beginning chemistry and physics, stemming from the group job and the subject matter of the year. But above and beyond this, the children became accustomed to trying out in the laboratory a process which interested them, seeking the answer to a question which came up in school or even in the home. It was not possible or desirable to lay before children of these ages more than the simplest of scientific material and some acquaintance with laboratory technique, although individual children occasionally went quite astonishingly far in their own researches. What the children as a group could and did absorb was the scientific method, the method of subjecting their ideas to the test of actual fact.

The trips never were abandoned. Children whose first learning was done by going out to see for themselves would never give up this method, especially now when it was so needful to them to keep their study of distant things alive and close, to tie together the past and the present.

We had seen how much more than mere information the children derived from their trips. They built up a reliance on their ability to seek and find what they needed. They became independent explorers in an environment, the details of which became every day more familiar to them. They became less conscious of mere facts and more aware of processes. They asked questions and found their own answers —if adults would let them. At every point they were establishing habits of thinking which would serve them for the rest of their lives.

One kind of thinking was to my mind so precious—and so elusive—that at a point in our growth I found myself more than a little troubled. So much had the discussions of subject matter absorbed us that I feared we were losing sight, with the older children, of what I must call creative activity.

More than any other part of our work, I think, parents have questioned our emphasis on painting, modeling, songs and stories and plays created by the children themselves. Particularly when their children have reached the upper school, parents have doubted the value of these activities even while they took pride in the children's creations. If we were not exclusively interested in turning out little Rembrandts and Shakespeares—as we firmly insisted we were not —what was the good of it all? A mother with her eye on a bank presidency was inclined to think we were wasting her son's time.

When I began to fear that our emphasis on subject matter and attention to academic techniques was depriving the older children of this kind of activity, it was a challenge to me to articulate something which had been implicit in our planning for children from the beginning. Even more than to our teachers (whom I had very little work to convince since they shared the same basic approach), this understanding is a necessity to parents.

Besides the kind of facts we consciously go out to discover, there is another body of facts we value which are beyond planning. Even as adults we are aware that a given experience may leave with us deeper impressions than we are conscious of, impressions which are stored away to emerge later when called upon, or which unconsciously color our thinking, even sway our decisions. When children go on trips, for example, they often absorb more than we see revealed or can even guess. These facts sometimes go to swell a fund of related information already there, or they may remain isolated facts until they are needed. We unconsciously draw upon these reserves for what Bergson called *intuitive thinking.*

On the wall opposite my desk hangs a picture painted by a child of seven. It is a block of city houses in beautiful colors. The windows are sometimes yellow and sometimes black, showing that it is time to light up for evening. The Elevated—familiar New York sight until a few years ago— is drawn across the whole scene, its pillars rising heavily black across the house-fronts. The child had recognized that the rails must be strengthened to carry their load of trains. She also saw the pillars in terms of form, and placed them in relation to the whole composition. There is snow on the ground; the smoke from all the chimneys is blowing in the same direction. There are cars on the street, an elevated train on the tracks—and this is not half of the evocative detail the picture contains.

This child did not know she knew all these things about a city street under the Elevated on a winter evening, until she needed them, and began to draw upon her secret store-house. Perhaps these stored-up facts had no relationship to each other, until the moment when her mind's eye, guiding her paint brush, called them forth and they fell into their places.

No, we have not been trying to encourage Rembrandts and Shakespeares. But we have tried to develop the whole of each child. Their paintings, sculptures, poems, and plays are important not as art or literature, but as exercises in this intuitive thinking as well as in logical thinking.

The child, sponge-like, stores up masses of such information below the surface of the mind. It is his way of catching up with the complex world he lives in; he takes in impressions at every pore, and what he cannot at once digest and use, he stores away for the future. A mother once told me she could not believe her little boy when he said he remembered his grandfather, who died when the child was two-and-a-half. But the boy described the old gentleman's way of walking, the smell of his cigar, his walking stick, even the suit in which the child had last seen him, details which the mother herself had not observed, which she confirmed with other relatives. This is only a spectacular example of what children do every day, every moment of their waking lives. They drink up impression, detail, fact. It is up to us, in planning a school program which will encourage such receptiveness, to provide situations which call upon these hidden stores of knowledge.

For the ability to absorb and then to call upon such knowledge is one of the gifts of childhood which are all too easily lost along the way to maturity. Artists try consciously to preserve it; they call it spontaneity, freshness, originality, inspiration. Art could not exist without it, but its importance is not only to art. Any contribution to man's progress in scientific discovery, in invention, in philosophic understanding owes something to this thinking which underlies the surface of the mind. An inventor or a scientist is always struggling to make the path smooth for an idea which he knows is there, under the thin cover of his logical thinking. When this idea emerges it may be the one he needs to complete the pattern of his work; if it is not, it is rejected by his logical thinking.

I have been asked by teachers who have met our graduates in the high schools, what has given these young people such vitality of interest and purpose and so much originality and imagination. If this is true of them, I am convinced that it is due to the opportunity they have had to develop intuitive thinking along with logical thinking, and that the opportunity has been found largely in the kind of work called "creative." Painting or modeling or story-writing or even dramatics may not interest an individual child. No matter—he will find what he needs, perhaps, in laboratory experiment, or in a problem in the shop, or in the print room. It is not the creative work itself—the art product—that we value, but the intuitive thinking upon which it calls.

Too much pressure of external ideas, too much preoccupation with mere skills and mere information, crowds out the elusive spark of original thought, dries up the stream of stored impressions. A little child who seems deliberately not to hear us when we say, "Do this," "Do that," who seems for the moment actually transported out of his own physical body, is protecting this inner process in which facts and impressions flow together into relationships as atoms flow into molecules. As he grows and is bombarded with demands for accomplishment by the conscious levels of his mind, he will lose this source of thinking which is so peculiarly his own.

If our school should ever forget this in striving after greater academic achievement—and what a temptation this is, what pressures must be resisted, I know all too well—it will lose what is to me its most important value to the development of children into complete human beings.

CHAPTER ELEVEN
PLAYS—
BY AND FOR CHILDREN

As THE CHILDREN, growing older, developed greater facility in the language arts, they tended more toward words in their creative activities. Painting, modeling, shop work fell into the background except for those children whose ideas continued to find a ready expression in the graphic arts.

One form of creative activity, however, united both the word-minded and the graphic-minded children in a group project which gave channels of expression to them all, one which swelled with increasing importance and interest as the children grew older: making a play.

This making of plays by children, as we have watched and encouraged its development, needs a word to itself. Some of our parents whose work or interests bind them to the theater world have questioned whether this kind of play is a play at all.

If a play can be defined as a dramatic product evolved by collaborative effort, with costumes, settings, properties, and actors performing as characters in a story, then these children's productions are plays. But if the concept depends on an audience for whose benefit or enjoyment the whole production is designed, then I am afraid our theater-minded parents are right. The children make their plays for nobody's benefit and enjoyment but their own.

True, they are eager for an audience, and demand permission to invite another group to the performance; most particularly they want to have their parents come to the play. They tack on the trimmings of the adult theater, with programs elaborately and often very beautifully designed by the children themselves. And they generally have an announcer or narrator, one of the cast who steps forward before and between the acts to introduce the characters and explain the action, and again rather quaintly at the end to tell the audience, in case they have missed the point, that the play is over.

This custom, I have often thought, was a sop to their guilty little consciences. For, having invited the audience, once the play is on they promptly ignore it, becoming so absorbed in their story and the enactment of it that they turn their backs and address their lines exclusively to each other, even to the scenery on the back wall, without a thought for those out front trying to catch their words. Their very physical arrangement is a giveaway: while they hang their scenery with a very good notion of where the stage ends and the audience begins, their action is likely to wander all over the Gym, and the audience finds itself squeezed against the wall, crowded onto the piano, all but pushed out of the room. By the time they are twelve or thirteen they have a feeling for the stage scene and stay within it, but when they are young all the world really is their stage; quite unawares, they appropriate every bit of space to themselves and their play.

No doubt the more familiar school production of a professionally written play, with the little actors speaking the lines they have learned by heart and constantly aware of the audience, is a smoother, slicker affair, with opportunities for virtuoso performances by the child actors which win them much applause. Perhaps such a play is more interesting to the adult spectators, though I doubt it with all my instincts. It may even be fun of a kind for the children who participate in it. But it just isn't "making a play" as we understand the phrase, or rather as we have been taught the meaning of the phrase by children themselves.

Children are forever play-acting. Little girls dress up in their mother's dresses and high-heeled shoes; little boys play Lone Ranger and Commando in the street. In a school which actually fostered this kind of play as part of the day's work, the delights of play-acting expanded and deepened before our eyes into one of the children's happiest ways of studying their lessons. As they learned about their world they gave it back in this richly satisfying group activity, pooling their knowledge of facts and their imaginative understanding of how things really were, in the near, present world about them or in the far-away or long-ago.

They play-acted from almost the earliest years. Even the youngest children liked to be bunnies or frogs hopping about the rhythms room, and in the beginning days of the school they were the babies of the family in games of playing house. They began consciously to make plays, however, when they were about seven; little girls perhaps showed the desire somewhat earlier, but no considerable group of a number was likely to say before this age, "Let's make a play." By the time they were eight the entire group understood the project of play-making, although some of them might still not be ready to take part.

How much a play was their own, how little the teacher or any adult injected grown-up ideas into their play-making, is clear from one play of the Nines which I remember for its unique scene-shifting arrangement. They had decided to have an outdoor play with the yard as their theater, and had pinned their backdrops to the fence, one for each scene— in effect a series of stages, with the cast going from one to another for each succeeding act. Only children, or persons to whom the conventions of the theater with its fixed stage and changing scenes were comparatively unknown, could have hit upon such an unconventional device.

To make a play together a group must have a common background of knowledge to work with. It might be a dramatic scene from the history they were studying, which they were moved to act out. A family making the westward trek in a covered wagon was a perennial favorite with the nine-year-olds, but no two groups of Nines made the same play out of the subject. Sometimes the play would begin in the rhythms period. One group whose interest had taken the sea-lanes rather than the land trails developed a most beautiful and impressive play out of an idea begun in rhythms: the gymnasium became a ship, sailing from port to port, touching distant lands, and the actors were sailors who clambered aloft on the ladder apparatus, sighting vessels and reporting on them in nautical language, while the captain shouted his orders from the deck. Sea chanties were sometimes sung, sometimes merely played by the accompanist as musical atmosphere for the action. When a port was reached, the people came out to greet the boat dressed in their native costumes, and proper cargoes were unloaded and loaded, whereupon the ship sailed on. In the end all the children formed themselves into a ship's outline, which dissolved as one by one they left the room.

What a mass of information, geographic, historic, and economic, went into the making of this play, only one who watched its unfolding, with a constant awareness of the children who had produced it, could truly grasp. This was the important thing about this kind of play-making—that the children were free to take over, from any and all fields of knowledge within their scope, whatever they needed in remaking into something of their own an incident or way of life which stimulated them.

The whole group are playwrights, stage managers, scene painters, costume designers and actors. In ingenuity and spontaneity, in the interpretation of situation and character, in humorous comment both conscious and unconscious, now and then sharp enough to make us adults squirm, such a play far outclasses the ready-made school production.

Best of all is the social experience of an effort so intensely collaborative. There is the constant offering and examining of ideas in the play's formulation, in the choosing of actors, in the designing and execution of settings and costumes, in the choice and the creation of music. The lines of a scene are not written down and are never spoken precisely the same way twice, but the actors agree on cues and on the content of a scene or a stretch of dialogue, and as it changes with each rehearsal the best is retained for the final performance. Adults who grasp the children's purposes in such a play, and who have the humility to accept their own very minor role as spectators, find these plays a revealing glimpse into the dramatic inner life of their children.

How a twelve-year-old group made a play, from the first

discussion of ideas to the finished product, is here narrated in notes by their teacher, Sybil May:

CHOOSING A SUBJECT

"In the fall of 1936 we began our history study with the situation then dominating the international scene—the war between Italy and Ethiopia. We tried to analyze the causes of the war, and in so doing studied a little about the Industrial Revolution, the growth of the British, French, and German Empires, and the World War. We used as our basic text Rugg's *Changing Civilizations*, which has excellent maps and graphs, as well as a clear, simple manner of presenting information. The geography involved in this study included, besides map work, a survey of the distribution of natural resources in European countries. This distribution, we found, was a factor in the industrial development of countries and in the struggle for colonies which came to a head in 1914. We studied especially the distribution of coal and iron, and of oil.

"When we came to the World War, I found the children keenly interested in the withdrawal of Russia from the war in 1917; so we went back again further into the past and studied about causes and the main events of the Russian Revolution. We had reached this point in March, when the children began working on original long stories as part of their work in creative writing. I assigned three choices of subject, all based on the war: 1) An English soldier returns home after the war to find his job in a mill has been taken and there is no work for him. 2) German and French coal miners in a Saar coal mine meet after the war is over. They were friends before the war, were parted by it, and have come together again. 3) A Russian peasant deserts and finds his way back to his village during the Russian Revolution. Of these themes the Russian was by far the most popular, and some of the stories were surprisingly vivid. Only one boy chose the coal mine subject.

"Early in April, when we met after spring vacation, we knew that the traditional moment had come for serious consideration of the subject of the play to be given at the end of the year. At discussion I asked each child to write down what he or she wanted the play to be about. Here is the list of their suggestions, exactly as they came and were written on the blackboard:

L. *Different scenes in Africa leading to the World War*
G. *Before and after the War*
H. *Russia during the Revolution*
Y. *One of our long stories*
E. *Exploring and settling the Gold Coast*
C. *The elevator strike*
T. *A play in the Chinese manner (no scenery)*
N. *A play of the mines in France and Germany*
W. *West Virginia mines, showing how badly off miners are*

"The remaining five children had either no suggestions or duplicated the above. During the discussion which followed, other suggestions developed: a dramatization of the life of Lenin; an adaptation of the movie about Cecil Rhodes in Africa; a play about the life of a striker and what he goes through; a play showing a fence along the French and German border (suggested by my description of the motion picture *Kameradschaft*, which is about an accident in a coal mine between France and Germany).

"Finally we took a vote, or rather a series of elimination votes, which resulted in a tie between a play about a mine on the border between France and Germany during the World War, and a play about the Russian Revolution. At this point I suggested that the seven coal miners go off and work out a sketchy dramatization of their theme, and the seven Russians do the same. Then each group would perform their play for the other and we would all know more about the potentialities of each theme. This suggestion met with an enthusiastic response. As judges, the student teacher and I were not allowed to help with either sketch, but became merely part of the audience.

"The coal mine had four scenes, all very brief of course, and not as yet in chronological order; simply indications of what the action might be. Following is a synopsis of the action:

SCENE 1. *In an inn soon after the Armistice. French and German miners talk a little about the war being over, and the dangerous condition of the mine.*

SCENE 2. *In the mine. A roof caves in. Pierre is left behind in the obstructed passage.*

SCENE 3. *In the war Germans and Frenchmen get into a fight, in the course of which a German kills a Frenchman. The dying Frenchman calls his son to his side and enjoins him always to hate Germans.*

SCENE 4. *Another cave-in. This time the German saves the Frenchman's son, who has sworn to hate all Germans.*

The Russian play had five scenes:

SCENE 1. *Peasants at work in the fields. A cruel overseer beats one of them until he dies.*

SCENE 2. *In a peasant's hut, showing how hungry peasants are.*

SCENE 3. *At a noble's house. A fierce discussion of how the peasants don't pay their tithes.*

SCENE 4. *At a peasant's house. A friendly overseer urges the peasants to join the Revolution and attack the noble's house.*

SCENE 5. *The attack. The friendly overseer is killed.*

"When we came to vote again, the result was that the seven coal miners were for their play and the seven Russian peasants for theirs. So we were not much better off. The student teacher and I finally broke the tie by deciding on the coal mine play, because it seemed to us that it had more dramatic possibilities. The Russians accepted the decision and cooperated wholeheartedly on the mine play.

PLANNING THE ACTION

"The next step was to plan the main action of the coal mine play. The complicated plot which finally developed was a result of trial and error. The chief objection to the try-out sketch was that a second cave-in was 'stale' and spoiled the climax. In fact, what we eventually retained of the original sketch was the main theme of the last scene—that if they feel that a war is not their own, workers will stand by each other even though their countries stand opposed. We agreed in the beginning that that was what we wanted our play to express, and in our planning we kept revising the plot in order to bring out this idea. We decided that a mine accident was the obvious way of showing workers helping each other in wartime, and we learned much about the dangers of mining in the course of our study of library books describing explosions, floods, fires, cave-ins, and poisonous gases. Besides the usual reference books, we used Pierre Hubermont's *Thirteen Men in a Mine.* It so happened that at this time the newspapers and radio were full of the fate of three men trapped in an abandoned mine in Nova Scotia.

"We finally decided upon the disaster we would dramatize: a flood plus exposure to the dread gas known as Black Damp. The reason for this selection was that I read aloud a vivid account of a flood from Cronin's *The Stars Look Down* (then just published; it was later made into a motion picture). The plot of this powerful book hinges upon an old map of a mine, which the mine owner secretly holds in his possession. Through his study of the map, he alone knows that a dangerously thin wall separates a particularly rich coal seam from a body of water behind it. Yet because of his desire for profits, he orders his men to work the seam. There is water behind the wall. The result is sudden and terrific disaster.

"The map idea seized the children's imagination, but they wanted also to bring in the war, so they hit upon the scheme of having the map of a border mine secretly altered by spies from the enemy country across the border, in order to cause a flood. This plot seemed to me complicated to get over to an audience, but the children were so intrigued by it that I let them go ahead. It did provide good suspense and a chance for the 'villain' that children always love. Sometime early in the construction of the plot the suggestion was adopted that we show the building of a wall in the mine to separate the French and German sides just before the outbreak of war (an idea derived from *Kameradschaft*).

"After many discussions and try-outs of different possibilities by small groups, a rough scheme finally emerged. This scheme was to have first an exposition scene; next the secret alteration of the map; then the flood and the rescue by the friendly workers from the enemy country.

"Now that the general plan of action was agreed upon, we could, at long last, cease talking about the play and start seriously 'acting out' the various scenes. We created the characters necessary to carry out the action outlined for a certain scene; children volunteered to 'be' those characters, and then went off by themselves to make up the dialogue and the 'business' that would fulfill the purpose of that scene in relation to the plot. When they were ready, they would play out the scene to the rest of the group, who would then evaluate it in terms of how it fitted into the play as a whole; whether or not it would be clear to the audience; how consistent the characters were in their acting and talk; and whether or not the scene was 'boring' (meaning all talk, no action).

THE ACTION

"The plot as finally worked out had many defects—but its authors were satisfied with it sufficiently to act it out with enthusiasm and conviction. The details are not important, but what is important is how the group drove home the main theme of the play: that the bond between workers of enemy countries can be stronger sometimes than the hostility imposed by a war which is not of their making. In order to bring this out, we created our main characters, two buddies, Hans the German and Pierre the Frenchman, who for years had been working together in a mine on the border between Germany and France.

"In the first act, we showed these two men working together in the mine, a week before the declaration of war. In their lunch hour, as they watch masons building a wall to separate the French from the German side of the mine, they talk about the imminence of war and the possibility of their being separated. A new worker, François, is brought in; he has been fired from a textile factory for organizing against the conversion of the factory into a munitions plant. His appearance provides the opportunity for the miners to tell him about general conditions in the mine: the low pay, the lack of a union, the danger from a thin wall, which is reported to have water behind it; also about disturbing new goings-on—the building of a new boundary wall, the sudden speed-up in the coal production. The new worker begins to protest against the preparations for war; he is interrupted by the entrance of the foreman and an army recruiting officer, who singles out the German from the French miners. This of course involves Hans and Pierre, the two buddies. Hans is ordered to quit because he is a German. Under the leadership of the new worker, Pierre and the others protest the firing of Hans, but they are not well enough organized and the curtain falls on the sorrowful parting of the two old friends.

"The second act, three years later, shows German Secret Service men plotting to alter a plan of the mine so that a new manager, who does not know the mine well, will order his men to work the seam with the water behind it, thus causing a flood which they hope will drown hundreds of French miners and ruin the mine.

"In the first scene of the third act, this comes to pass. Some of the men are drowned; others perish from the Black Damp. Only a few escape, led by Pierre up a shaft which rises above flood level to the wall, which in the first act was built between the French and German sides of the mine.

"The last scene, two days after the flood, shows the German side of the mine where the unsuspecting Hans and his companions are eating their lunch and talking depressedly about the weary duration of the war. Suddenly they hear tapping on the wall. Hans strains his ears and finally hears faint calls for help. He hears or thinks he hears his name. He immediately guesses what has happened, and of course stops his lunch. The other miners run to the adjoining chamber to get help.

"Meanwhile the foreman enters and an argument ensues. Hans wants to rescue his old buddy, Pierre, on the French side of the mine. The foreman wants the men to go back to work and ignore the cries for help. The soldier insists that he will not allow the wall which he is guarding to be broken down. Finally they resort to blows and Hans and a fellow miner throw out the foreman and the soldier. Then the other miners who have come in begin battering on the wall with feverish haste. At last a breach is made and Pierre is pulled through. He is exhausted from exposure and the Black Damp, and the rescue comes too late. He dies in the arms of his old buddy. But before he dies he manages to gasp his message, 'We can't stop this war, but maybe, if we stick together, maybe we can stop the next.'

DIALOGUE

"The children did not memorize their lines; in fact most of the lines were never written down. This does not mean that good lines were not repeated often enough to be counted on in the final performance; nor does it mean that we could not count on cues. On the contrary, a scene was sometimes gone over so often, and a certain order of speakers and speeches was so important to the action, that the dialogue was pretty well crystallized. But it does mean that every child varied his lines somewhat and sometimes improvised new ones in the final performance.

"Discipline and freedom were combined. The order of development was fixed, the actual wording flexible, with the sole provision that the necessary point be made. Occasionally an actor would write down an important speech and ask the group to criticize it. The critics cut it out if it was not in character, or if it impeded the action. Children who have had practice in making their own plays become wary of too much talk, and of lines that sound unreal or bookish.

"The last scene, taken down in shorthand at the final performance, is here presented as characteristic of the terseness of the dialogue all the way through:

ACT III, SCENE 2: *German mine.*

(*Hans and Fritz are eating their lunch; a soldier is sitting near by.*)

HANS: Ain't got much lunch today.

FRITZ: No, and everything's stale!

HANS: My God, yes!

FRITZ: But it's better than nothing.

HANS (*looking at soldier*): Why in God's name aren't you in uniform?

SOLDIER: I'm not going to wear it in this blooming place!

(*Enter foreman*)

FOREMAN: Get to work, you guys!

FRITZ: We're eating!

FOREMAN: Get to work anyway. Five minutes is enough to have; you have time for breakfast, supper—what more do you want?

MEN: No we don't. (*They rise grumbling, go to work. Exit foreman.*)

HANS: I wish we'd get paid!

FRITZ: And when we do get paid it's by the amount we get out, and not by the time we work.

HANS: I wish this war was over!

FRITZ: They call it the World War now, a pretty good name for it, I'd say!

(*Re-enter foreman*)

FOREMAN: Say, you guys, get together; I have some orders here. You've got to do twice as much work this month as last. Hurry now, and get to work! If I come again and find you napping, we'll fire you!

(Men start to work again. A noise is heard; it sounds like tapping.)

HANS: Hey, what's that?

SOLDIER: Say, what's eating you?

HANS: There's nothing wrong with me—listen to that! What is it? I hear a voice. *(A muffled cry is heard from the other side of the wall.)* Fritz, drop your pick and listen!

SOLDIER: Don't pay any attention to what that guy's doing.

FRITZ: That's Pierre—he's calling something!

SOLDIER: It doesn't matter. *(More cries are heard.)*

HANS: It *is* Pierre! We must do something! *(Soldier tries to keep them from the wall. Foreman suddenly enters. Hans and Fritz knock him out.)*

SOLDIER: What have you done now?

HANS *(looking down at foreman)*: I don't know.

SOLDIER: I'll have to arrest you now. *(More cries are heard through the wall.)*

FRITZ: Whatever you do now will get you in trouble, Hans.

HANS *(listening)*: That's Pierre. I've worked with him ever since I worked in the mines. *(Starts towards wall again.)*

SOLDIER *(trying to keep them away from the wall)*: I'll have to arrest you. I like you, but my job comes first. Whatever my job is, I have to do it.

HANS: If you had a friend in there yelling for you, wouldn't you try to help him? Call the other miners, Fritz.

FRITZ: What are you going to do?

HANS: I'm going to break down the wall. *(More cries for help.)*

SOLDIER: Before you break down the wall, you'll have to kill me! I like you guys, but it's my duty to stop you.

(The miners start for the wall.)

SOLDIER: Get away from the wall! *(He tries to hold them away by force. Hans struggles with him; the soldier is overcome. As he falls, he fires his gun, killing Fritz.)*

(Enter the other miners. They start to work on the wall where the cries are coming from. They finally break through and drag Pierre out, half dead from exposure to gas and water.)

HANS: Pierre, Pierre, what happened?

PIERRE: Ugh, ugh *(choking and groaning)*. Water, flood,

Black Damp. (*Chokes again.*)

HANS: What happened to François?

PIERRE (*choking*): Lost . . . drowned . . . ugh, ugh. Guys were working bad wall. I told them not to . . . ugh, ugh . . . but they did.

HANS: Couldn't François help you?

PIERRE: Yes . . . he . . . he did, but the foreman wouldn't listen. François said we should stick together. He said we couldn't stop this war . . . but maybe . . . maybe we could stop the next one. Ugh . . . ugh . . . oh . . . (*Pierre dies.*)

HANS (*seeing that his friend is dead*): Oh, oh . . . my best friend . . . Pierre. (*Then turning to the others*) O.K. guys, we *will* stick together, won't we?

MEN: Yes, yes, we *will* stick together.

(*Curtain*)

CASTING: EFFECT ON THE CHILD

"My experience has been that it is better to stave off the casting for the final performance as long as the group will allow you to. Their desire is to have the parts decided right away in the beginning. The advantage of this is that the main characters (and there should be as many main characters as possible) will have a chance to develop their parts according to their wishes. The disadvantage is that few children then have the experience of identifying themselves with any part that is convenient at a particular moment. This flexibility is one of the most important advantages of the created play as against the ready-made, and for this reason I insist upon it until the play's action is pretty well crystallized.

"Another reason for continually shifting parts is that often a child benefits by being asked to take on temporarily a character with whom he is not in sympathy. Understanding of people is necessary for any group. A play is an excellent beginning of that understanding. I am frank to say I engineered the casting as diplomatically as I could in order to accomplish my ends and still give the feeling that this play was the children's, not mine. I had several psychological axes to grind. I wanted to make W. and L. understand, through emotional experience rather than through cold information, just what workers are up against. I wanted C. and D., hitherto nonentities, to register with the group. I wanted to give H., who had a gift for clowning, and who was already established as a serious thinker, an opportunity to contribute to the play the necessary comic relief. I wanted to prevent the glib talkers from monopolizing the play.

"I cannot claim to have ground all these axes—not in one play. But this much the play did accomplish psychologically. W., who is a very efficient worker herself and scornful of people who don't throw themselves into work hard, did learn, through acting the part of a too submissive worker, that it is one thing to be a little girl in a home and school which devote all their skill to providing the right work environment, and another to be a worker for a company which devotes all its skill to extracting the greatest possible profit from a worker. C. as Pierre and D. as the new manager both turned out to be excellent actors and won the respect of their group. H. extended her facility for providing humor appreciated by both adults and children. None of the children monopolized the play at any point.

"So much for the successes. Now for the failures. L. never really developed an identification with the workers, though I tried him in every worker's part. The actor remained always the superior intellectual—a philosopher above the battle. R. could not stop clowning long enough to develop any part; and in the end, in order not to risk his spoiling the play, we gave him a minor part as mason. G. I am not sure about. He is a shy boy who, though he has realistic convictions, is usually a sheepish follower, never a leader. In the play we made him act the organizer. He saw the job through, but whether the experience developed.in him any confidence in an ability to lead in a real struggle, I am doubtful."

CHAPTER TWELVE

DEMOCRACY IN MINIATURE

ONE OF OUR teachers brought me a six-year-old one day whose behavior perplexed her. He had been disrupting the group by hitting the children, one after another, without visible cause. The boy was new to the school.

The children perform
in plays...

...and make music.

Enjoying "yard" and science...

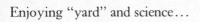

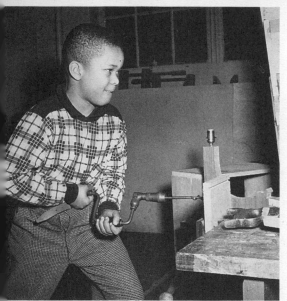

...and shop—
where Caroline began!

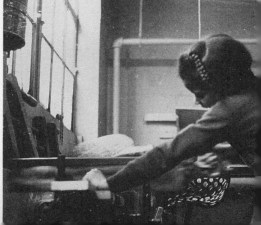

I asked him what the trouble was, and he took command of the situation at once.

"It's like this, Miss Pratt—I hit a child and he hits me, then we know each other. Don't stop me now, Miss Pratt. I've hit them all but two, and if you'll just let me finish, you won't have any more trouble with me!"

There are ways and ways of getting along with our fellows, and this little boy's way was only one of them. Nor was it by any means the worst. Many a child tries to buy his way with gifts, money, almost any kind of concession. Big boys have been known to do the same, and with approximately the same success. Appeasement can lead to no good end.

There are only two honest ways to deal with an antagonist. Either you come to an understanding, or—as a last resort—you fight. Our little six-year-old was merely reversing the order of things by fighting first and reaching an understanding afterward.

Which way you try first makes some slight difference. All over the world there are people of good will trying to make mankind take the understanding way first. It would seem that if there were enough men and women in the world who had learned from childhood how to work toward an understanding, how to go about reconciling apparently conflicting interests, then perhaps it would no longer come to fighting.

That this is an oversimplification of the monstrous agonies the world is suffering I am willing to concede at once. But all the people in the world were children once, and for the origin of most good or bad ways of doing things we must go back to childhood—for the origin of social reactions, back to birth. One can almost predict, from the impact of a baby's first cry, whether his social relations are to be happy ones. How his mother receives his first vocal demand is a reasonably clear omen of his future. If he is unwanted, or wanted for the wrong reasons, he is already off to a bad start, and his way will be a hard one.

If his mother loves him, if she offers him the simple respect which one human being owes to another human being however small and helpless, he is a lucky child. For him the world will have a friendly face, because the one on whom he first depended has tried to understand him. A good mother need not be gifted, or beautiful, or even very clever; she is a good mother if she offers her child understanding.

But no child has gone far who has merely come to terms with his mother; there are many other relationships with which he must deal, and the good mother helps him by setting him gradually free among his equals. Unlike his mother, these small strangers are utterly uninterested in finding out what he wants; they care only about what they want, and how to get it. He learns to defend himself, to fight if necessary, but chiefly he learns how to get along with his contemporaries. This first step in his emancipation from the home is enormously important in the pre-school years. If he already has healthy relationships at home, and is allowed to make his way with his own kind outside the home, he is well on his way to becoming a happy citizen of the community.

Now comes school—and this happy little citizen, this naturally gregarious little individual, finds himself in a strange world where an entirely different kind of behavior is expected of him. He cannot make friends with his teacher, who has thirty or forty other children to look after (sometimes more, be it said to the shame of our public school systems). He dare not pass the time of day with his neighbor; now suddenly this is bad behavior, and he will be punished. If he is not willing to be cowed, if he shows a spirit of curiosity or playfulness, he is "anti-social." Mere friendliness is a disturbance. Whatever else he may learn in a formal school, he will not learn to live with others, for the system enjoins him strictly to go his own way and mind his own business.

Fortunately he spends only six hours of his day in this curious confinement. There are still daylight hours when, if he is lucky, he can play with other children in the park or his backyard, or even in the street. But he is only comparatively lucky. Though he is free to play, there is no one to help him and his friends to get the most out of their play together, to show them ways of planning together for the good of the whole group, of settling disagreements, of understanding each other. All too often the bloody-nose method becomes the only one to end an argument.

I don't think I overstate the failure of the traditional schools in ignoring this part of a child's learning. Some of them are beginning to realize this responsibility, and to make tentative efforts toward a "socialized curriculum." With standardized systems and, above all, classes and schools that are always too large, it is uphill work.

Life in school is only another setting for life anywhere. If we were preparing our children to live under an autocratic regime I could understand the need for iron discipline, for suppression of playfulness and friendliness, of adventure or individualism wherever it raises its head. But we are preparing our children to be responsible citizens in a democracy, perhaps some day in a democratic world. Why then the screwed-down benches, the interdiction on speech, the marching through the halls in silent single-file, the injunction on the teacher to behave like a classroom Hitler?

With us the emphasis was, from the beginning, completely reversed. The program of work and play, the very physical aspect of the classrooms, was planned not only to encourage but indeed to use the child's natural eagerness to join with other children in most of his activities. We never doubted that conversation was as natural in school as at home or on the playground; we assumed that school was as good a place as any to learn that there were times for listening as well as for talking, that a discussion gets nowhere if everyone talks at once, that your neighbor—and even your teacher—once in a while has something to say which you would do well to hear.

Since we believed in young children learning through play, we prepared for them a classroom free of desks, with blocks and toys and clay and drawing materials on open shelves for all to use in common. There were tables where children could work together sociably if they wished, other tables somewhat apart where a child could work alone who wanted or needed privacy. Each child had his own things, too: the locker where he hung his clothes was his, with his name on it, and above it was a compartment where he could keep the things he was making by himself. The first lesson in social living is to distinguish between that which belongs to everyone and that which is one individual's alone. Such a classroom provided daily graphic demonstration of the lesson in terms which even the youngest children could grasp.

It would be next to impossible to talk of any aspect of the school's work without reference to the social experience which is automatically a part of it; as in life itself, the individual is always both an individual and a member of a group. We have seen how a shy and retiring child may be drawn into making a real contribution to the group; how confidence in oneself and appreciation of others' work are built up in the daily sharing of work and play; especially how cooperation in the school service jobs develops in the individual child a sense of responsibility to the group and to the school as a whole: surely this is a way of learning to be future citizens of a democracy.

But it would be a false picture of human endeavor, however young, if we assume that these embryo citizens functioned together in unfailing sweetness and light. There was no lack of opportunity for learning to understand one's neighbor, even on the very youngest levels. The snatched toy, and the quick blow or howl of protest which followed, gave the teacher her chance to point up the lesson in its most elementary form.

To a young child, the obvious way to get what you want is to take it, and in the Nursery School that method was constantly being attempted. Sometimes the snatcher learned his lesson directly, when the toy was snatched back with a slap or a push to make the lesson stick. When the fracas was over and it was clear that the snatch method had got him nowhere, he had a chance to state his case.

If it was really a question of the toy itself, a solution was rarely difficult. A young boatbuilder, who really needed a block of a certain size and tried to get it by snatching, was willing enough to examine the situation with the teacher when his first method failed. Was there another such block on the shelf? Could the second boy spare the block without running into trouble in his bridgebuilding? Yes—two short blocks could replace the one long one which the boatbuilder needed. It was then up to the boatbuilder to convince the bridgebuilder, and if there was no other, subtler cause for dissension the whole case was settled to everyone's satisfaction.

The subtler causes are complications to which the teacher must be alert. Sometimes the block has not been the issue at all; the aggressor has actually wanted to pick a quarrel. Such a child is not ready for the immediate lesson of getting on with his fellows. He needs to come to terms with himself first. Temporary isolation helps him to realize that his behavior has not been acceptable, and at the same time gives him the chance, by working alone, to turn his energies into a productive channel and to give him a successful achievement of his own in blocks or paints or clay, a beginning toward that inner security and self-confidence which are the basis for good social relations.

Because there is no rule against fighting, there is no reason to assume that all problems have to be settled by the contenders themselves and therefore by force. If we are trying to lay a foundation for thinking, in living as well as in learning, we must use every available opportunity to help a child toward understanding what another individual is about, toward finding out what is in the other's mind. It would be absurd to expect very young children to go far with such an effort, but it is possible to begin while they are young, and a teacher or parent who is both alert to her opportunities and patient in the use of them can make gratifying progress.

Even our youngest children have demonstrated a kind of social thinking of spontaneous—sometimes slightly dubious—origin. There was Polly who at two-and-a-half already had a Tom Sawyer technique for getting what she wanted. She tried snatching the attractive toy from Joan, without success. So she went to a shelf, chose another toy, toddled back to a spot close to Joan and began playing with it. Soon Joan lost interest in her own toy and abandoned it for Polly's—whereupon Polly seized the prize and made off with it! Polly's method worked, and with a certain rough justice, but it could be successful only as long as her playmates were innocent enough to be duped. Eventually Polly would have to develop into an honest trader.

More subtle still was Helen's handling of a social situation. Helen, just turned three, was sitting at a table, serenely making little objects of her own design out of plasticine. Came another little girl, who sat down beside her. "I don't like Helen," began the second child. "Nobody likes Helen, do you, Johnny?" Helen went on with her work for a while. Then she wrapped her bit of oilcloth around her plasticine, rose to her feet, said to her tormenter, "Helen likes herself," and betook herself to a vacant place between two other children. This was quite the most effective behavior that could have been devised.

Still, violence is sometimes an inevitable expression of childhood, and on occasion it has been best to let two contestants fight it out on the schoolroom floor. Here is the time when the teacher must use her judgment and her knowledge of the children concerned. One seven-year-old's mother told me how her boy, a shy youngster and new to the school, had to fight his way to friendship with one after another of the boys in his group. He was a sturdy child without any wish to fight but with the brawn to fight well once he was forced to it; he suffered no damage—children, evenly matched, rarely do—and gained what was to him an invaluable new self-confidence. The school yard provided for this lad, in safety, the toughening experience of the street which underprivileged children have as a matter of course. In his case it was good nourishment for his ego.

A ten-year-old class was once terrorized by three "gangsters" in their group who would meet the children one by one outside the school and threaten a beating. The real difficulty was that the rest of the group was cowed and felt defenseless before the use of force. So we began a course of training in self-defense for the group, excepting the gangsters; we engaged a boxing teacher to come in twice a week and give them lessons. I shall never forget one young miss who suddenly became a pugilist of killer quality the moment she put the boxing gloves on; in her new-found confidence the rules of the ring had no importance to her, and our problem became one not of encouragement but of restraint.

Soon we had a group of spirited youngsters who were willing to stand and fight the attackers. The group of three, like all such groups, had a cowardly streak in them. They too clamored for boxing lessons, but the answer they got was that they already knew how to fight and we could not waste the lessons on them. The reign of terror died a natural death.

Both kinds of treatment are essential in settling childish quarrels, in showing children the way to good social relationships. A child cannot be left helpless because of fear. Before he can put into use his ability to think things through and arrive at an understanding of his fellow, so that he can meet his antagonist halfway, his fear must be dispelled. The boxing lessons served this purpose; they dispelled the physical fear which dominated a child confronted with the three menacing "bandits." If he turned and ran, the pack was on him at once. But if he was not afraid, he could stand and think. He then had a choice of action: he could yell for help, or go to a policeman on the corner, or show a disposition to fight. Freedom to fight is not the solution, but freedom from fear.

What is surprising, perhaps, is the fact that the attacker, no less than the attacked, may be possessed by fear. It is not difficult to recognize that the timid child is afraid. The puzzling truth is that the child who attacks the timid one is quite as fearful as his victim. This is when children need a friend; it is also when fighting is the poorest of answers.

The timid child can be helped to dispel his fears, one by one. Success in his work and play enterprises brings him the respect of his peers and a double dose of tonic to his self-confidence, achievement and recognition. He can be made to grasp the possibility that his persecutor is afraid, too. What about facing him and finding out? I have known a teacher to work for weeks, to give a bully a much-needed lesson and help a timid child break through his fears.

The bully himself is much more challenging. To call him a bully neither explains nor helps him. His may be a deeply personal emotional difficulty, and I am far from claiming that social discipline of the kind I have been advocating can solve everything. A child who shows the traits of a bully may be a child in desperate need of help, even of psychiatric help. When the best efforts of teachers and parents together fail to free him from the troubles which drive him to unsocial behavior, there is no time to lose in seeking out the most expert help.

The children themselves understand each other far better than one would dare to expect. In a school where they are learning to use their freedom under careful guidance, they show astonishing perception and understanding of each other.

I watched a group of nine-year-olds play baseball one day. One boy constantly excused his failures by accusations against the others—they were unfair, they broke a rule, they lost the game by poor playing—all at the top of his voice. When the yard period was ended I discovered I had an errand for him, and in his absence I asked the other children why they put up with such behavior.

"Why, Miss Pratt, you don't understand Joe," one little girl said reproachfully. "Joe is always that way. We just pay no attention to him. That's the only way we can get along with him."

Here was a fine practical analysis of a particular situation, as far as it went. But it did not go far enough to be of any social value. An older group might have been induced to accept more responsibility for Joe—for what would become of him in a different group, one which did not know him, which would not give him this kind of consideration? This is another face of the problem of social learning, the responsibility of the group toward its members.

If Joe's difficulty had not been acute we might have worked that out, too. As it happened, the story of Joe had a really touching sequel, which in its way revealed that the group was in fact developing such responsibility. Joe's problems had become so serious that he was under the care of a psychiatrist. So well had the children made a place for him, problems and all, in their number, that he was able to talk about his visits to his doctor quite freely with them. There were times when he stayed out of school for days because he was emotionally upset; during such periods, all the children were concerned for him.

After one of these absences, rather longer than usual, the teacher watched the children carefully, curious to see their behavior on his return.

Not one child commented on his absence; they accepted him as though he had not been away. But it presently became clear that they were only waiting for the right moment. In the baseball game that morning, Joe had the good luck to make a fine hit. At once one of the boys rushed up to him and threw his arms about him, and the whole group, as if this were the cue to give vent to long pent-up feelings, gathered round with joyous congratulations. The sensitive understanding they had shown in waiting for this moment was as amazing as their quick recognition of it—a unanimous response—when it arrived.

With the older children we created special opportunities to exercise this surprisingly mature understanding. For several years I made the experiment of dividing the thirteen-year-old classes into sections and assigning each section to a group of little ones in the Nursery School. They observed behavior and then reported their interpretations to me. No specific assignments were made, but the young psychology students themselves often chose to observe the problem child in a group.

I was in the gymnasium one day with such a section of Thirteens, observing a five-year-old group at Rhythms. One small girl remained lying on the floor long after all the other children were on their feet. I asked each of my observers why the child did this. All three replied that she was showing off, bidding for attention.

I never had a class of student teachers who were more capable of discovering what lies back of certain types of behavior than these thirteen-year-old children. They were quick to grasp, too, that a child bidding for attention, as was the five-year-old on the gymnasium floor, was not following a growth pattern, that this kind of behavior led up a blind alley.

After our discussions we read the teachers' reports on the children they had observed, and when they found some of their own conclusions verified they were proud little psychologists. For most of them this kind of work was as interesting as anything else they did; it even competed successfully with baseball.

These children gave me such definitions as: "Psychology is what people do and deciding why they do it," and "Behavior is everything a person does," and, of the difference between behavior and conduct, "Conduct is good or bad behavior."

Their grasp of the elusive principles of human behavior was in every way astonishing, and I became convinced of their ability to go further and apply their discoveries to the problems which arose in their own groups, even in their own personal lives. There is really no reason to save psychology for college years; such studies, begun as we began them with thirteen-year-olds, and continued in high school, would do more to prepare children for solving future social problems than any amount of time spent on so-called Social Studies.

In one of our discussions—this with the entire group of Thirteens—the young observers were able, with help, to divide the children they had watched into two groups: those who responded to a drive within themselves, and those who depended on a stimulus from outside, such as attention or applause, to make them function.

Then, with malice aforethought, I turned their attention to their own group. They analyzed each member of the group, and were quick to see that some of them were working constantly under their own powerful drives. They agreed, however, that there was one outstanding exception among them, one who had no strong drives for work, who seldom forgot himself in what he was doing. The other children, they decided, fell somewhere between the self-forgetful and the self-conscious, with drives for work and desire for attention, too, varying with the individual.

In all this talk, and there was much of it, the children carefully refrained from naming the one boy who was outstanding in his self-consciousness and need for attention. All at once the boy himself spoke up—and it was gratifying not only that he could speak up at all, but that he could speak in the same objective, scientific tone about himself.

"I know it," he said, reassuring them, "I know it and I'd rather die than not be the center of attention."

Yes, we make a mistake when we underestimate children's understanding of their own and each other's frailties. And if we think they are blind even to our adult shortcomings, we are living in a fool's paradise. It is an illusion reserved for parents and teachers that we can cover our faults from their innocent eyes with a garment of omnipotence and omniscience. Those eyes are not so innocent as we choose to think. A very young child learns of necessity how to protect himself from a mother's quick temper, a father's business-weary irritability; he feels the threat, though his protective devices do not always protect him well enough.

They see and hear much more than we give them credit for, and sometimes even can put their observations into words. Here, for example, is a conversation among three children, overheard and recorded without editing by a student teacher.

Evelyn: "Tommy, I don't like your mother."
Sue: "Why don't you like his mother?"
Evelyn: "Because there's no kindness inside."
Tommy: "But how did *you* know that? You should see how she treats my father!"

I have yet to meet a parent who could hear this fragment of dialogue without starting; I have even discerned a fleeting expression of fear. We are right to be afraid. These children, who are at our mercy, are well aware of our power over them, and aware too of the things in us which can do them harm. There's little sense in our saying to them, "Now be a good child." Better for us to say to each other, "Be a good adult."

CHAPTER THIRTEEN

A TEACHER COOPERATIVE

I DID NOT DREAM, when I first gathered around me a group of six children in the apartment on West Thirteenth Street, that this small beginning would grow in the next thirty years into a full nursery and elementary school caring for children from three through thirteen.

Nor would I have dared to hope that it would become, as one of our many distinguished parents has described it, "an experiment under a glass dome . . . reaching toward an end that the tested residue of the work could be applied to the vast areas of public education."

Certainly I have believed too deeply in the right of children to grow and learn in the ways that are true for children not to wish that others besides the two hundred who have worked and played within our walls each year could enjoy the same right, that other teachers besides our staff of twenty-odd would dedicate themselves to the cause of rescuing children from the dead hand of traditional education.

And I hope I can be forgiven for my pride in two public schools which are the direct offspring of City and Country School, the creations of our own staff—P. S. 33 in the slums of New York, and the Putnam Valley School which stands on a lovely hill above the farmlands of the Hudson River Valley. These, so different from City and Country and from each other in their setting, in the children whom they serve and the way of life into which they are fitted, are robust evidence that what is good for our children is good for children everywhere and of every kind, children who have apple trees to climb as well as children who carry the door key of a tenement flat on a string around their necks.

As I look back I see now that the principle of freedom for children always carried with it in my own thinking another freedom, freedom for teachers. Very early in the school's life, indeed from the first day when there was no longer merely a teacher—myself—but a staff, we worked on the principle that the teacher must have the freedom of her own classroom. Our regular and frequent staff meetings thrashed out general principles and specific problems, but always the teacher herself was responsible for what went on in her own group.

There is just one mechanism that can produce a unified, integrated piece of work: the human mind. No poem or painting, no philosophical system, no scientific theory was ever produced by a committee. Many minds may have contributed to each of these, but in the end one mind has gathered the ideas, the information, the logic and the creative imagination of many to make the vital, functioning whole.

And so, while we continually beat out our ideas together, tested our findings and our theories on each other, in the end it was the teacher who applied the principles, put the theories into practice, verified the findings by her own experience. The teacher in her classroom was the scientist in the laboratory and the artist in the studio, rolled into one, and supreme in her own sphere. It could not be otherwise.

Out of this way of working there emerged a kind of cooperative organization for the school, educationally speaking. Roughly the same form came into being for the school's administration. Very early we formed a teacher's committee on salaries to make a survey of other schools and recommend to the group a salary scale, including my own salary as principal, as well as minimum and maximum teacher salaries and annual increases.

Thus in theory we as the staff had taken on financial responsibility for the school. It was an easy decision to make in those days of small beginnings. The idea of an outside Board of Trustees was of itself a threat to the freedom which we cherished for our work—and where was the need? We were too small, too modest a group to require the services of lawyers, bankers, even accountants.

We scarcely guessed what a portentous decision we had made. I soon discovered, however, that while the teachers were willing to concern themselves briefly each year with the school budget, and to agree on salaries which were distinguished by their Spartan modesty, they were hard to interest in purely administrative functions.

I needn't have been surprised. The routine duties of administration could not be interesting when things were going smoothly, and where nothing was concealed. Teachers who had a corner of their own where they were supreme—the classroom—found their satisfactions within this little realm. Wholly absorbed in the creation of her own little community within the school, her group within the larger group, the teacher had little time or thought for a problem like rising food costs in the lunchroom or a breakdown in the heating system—so drearily dull compared with her group's suddenly blossoming interest in the causes of the American Revolution or the construction of a steam engine!

There is no doubt in my mind that, early in the school's life, I "ran the school" pretty much as I wished. I saw the teacher's function within her classroom as the development of a little community which worked as a unit around a chosen activity—and I saw my own function as principal in watching over the pattern of the school as a whole, keeping it flexible and making room for new ideas within its framework.

I know I was accused of accepting no one's idea until I had forgotten who offered it and then coming out with it as my own! Perhaps the accusation was justified. But where ideas came from seemed to me then, as now, less important than their value as ideas and their usefulness to the large idea of a school which we were working so hard to develop. I carried about a conception of the school, functioning as a whole, and I held myself responsible, in the final judgment, for its administration and its educational policy, no matter how many others—good teachers, lively and creative minds— contributed to it.

There came a time—a hard time—when the teachers, whom I had failed to interest in the administration of the school while things were going well, answered the call for help when the school needed them. Long before that time, however, when we moved to the Twelfth Street buildings, we found ourselves no longer the little group we had been, too small to attract anybody's attention, but a school of quite respectable dimensions, with responsibilities which made it essential that we take out incorporation papers with the Regents of New York State.

We wanted to incorporate as a teacher organization, and as Lucy Sprague Mitchell, the main financial support of the school, was not only willing but had made the suggestion herself, there were no barriers. Our lawyer, Timothy Pfeiffer, who was also a parent in the school, would have found it a much easier task to give us a regulation paper constitution and by-laws—which would have hampered us to the end of our days. Instead he considered the organization we had already worked out worthy of preservation.

The corporation as he set it up called for five charter members, and Mrs. Mitchell, a very active member of the staff, and four other teachers took these posts. Each year the corporation would elect the principal, secretary, and treasurer of the school as its own president, secretary and treasurer, respectively, and would accept as its board of directors the annually elected executive committee of the school. Thus happily the school was incorporated without disturbing what had already been set up and found workable.

Also provided, at our joint insistence, was an iron-bound condition that no individual should ever derive financial profit from the school. The corporation was instructed by the same paper which created it, that, if ever the time came when it must dissolve itself, the school properties or their proceeds must be devoted to a similar institution dedicated to the education of children.

The incorporation, so impressive on paper, made no difference in the school at first. Full of enthusiastic plans for making the richest use of our new plant, the teachers continued to give only the dregs of their attention, a rather bored acquiescence, to our periodic business meetings.

But the crisis came in the depression years, and it was then we discovered the profound value of a cooperative which had grown so naturally out of our common beliefs and our shared philosophy of education. Contributions dropped, tuitions dwindled, partial scholarships and full scholarships began to fill the registration book. The staff, confronted with real administrative problems, shouldered the new burdens, and business meetings came to grim life. Every expenditure came under sharp examination; ways of bolstering the school's income became everyone's responsibility. They even regarded their own modest salaries with a newly critical eye, and voluntarily decided to cover the increasing number of free tuitio is by deferring a portion of their salaries each year until better times. The school is still, with the help of its parents, paying back that debt to its teachers, the debt which was incurred for children whose parents could not pay for them.

Since then the staff have continued to work on committees which carry every substantial administrative responsibility, and I have no doubt they will eventually revolutionize the administration of the school. The main body of teachers are so closely identified with the school's fundamental philosophy that they can find the solutions to new situations without conflict. When our science teacher resigned at a time of serious deficit, we decided to economize on the salary of a new one and see whether each teacher could provide the science program for his or her own group. Surprising resources were revealed among us, and a science program was developed for every class, with a small sum of money reserved for a specialist to come in and do laboratory work with the older children.

As the economic storm abated, the cooperative has continued to function, a live group of teachers owning their own school and meeting its administrative problems. So far they have resisted one of the great pressures of our time and one of my own aversions, the pressure to grow too big. The temptation to add a high school, to increase the size of the present nursery and elementary schools, is ever present. But just as there is a limit to the size of each group—and it is a limit decided not by the size of the classroom space alone—so there is a limit to the size of a school if freedom for children, and for the creative imagination of teachers, is our ideal. And so, I ardently hope, it may always remain.

Never believe it was easy for me to give up my active responsibility for the school and retire as Principal Emerita! Not a bit easier than for any parents to learn to respect the independence of their adolescent children and rejoice in their ability to make their own decisions and run their own lives. What gives me the greatest confidence for the future is that I have seen these teachers in whose hands the school remains, learning from the children as I learned myself, making sacrifices of a very real and painful kind to maintain in hard times as well as good the standards to which we have all pledged ourselves. They cannot, as I cannot, look upon our school as a static achievement merely to be preserved. As I saw it in its earliest formative days, they continue to see it as a living organism, with a vitality of its own, putting forth new growth to meet the needs of children in their own time.

CHAPTER FOURTEEN

THE EDUCATION
OF PARENTS

I HAVE BEEN accused to my face of hating parents, of wishing all children could be born orphans. I have been told that when I saw a mother coming down the street I would walk clear around the block to avoid her. Fathers have consistently referred to themselves in my presence as Mere Fathers. They have professed themselves the most oppressed group of people in modern times, their shyly whispered opinions over-ridden, their hesitant questions brushed aside. What a calumny! I cannot imagine a group of parents who could be more hand-in-glove, more co-conspiratorial with the staff, more conversant with the principles and intimate with the processes of a school than the parents of the City and Country School have been.

The very title of this chapter is a libel on them, or at the least misleading. We have not educated parents. If they have been educated they have done the educating themselves. Or they have been educated as we have, by the children. In three decades we have all, parents and staff, done a good deal of learning, and those of us who are still with the school are learning still.

The accusation that I avoided parents is, however, at least partly true. In the early years I did many times walk around the block so as not to meet them, for the truth was hat I was afraid of them. They might well ask me what we were doing with their children—there were times when the question would find me hard put for an answer. If they wanted to know whether we were preparing them for high school I could not truthfully reassure them that we were; I could only say I hoped so. If they asked when their children would learn to read—*whether* they would learn to read was the way some put it—my answer again was more likely to alarm than comfort them.

For my own part I was afraid that they would get in our

way, that they would attempt to curtail our freedom of action, try to steer us closer to the more familiar, more comfortable kind of school. I was too deeply involved in the work in progress to stop and justify what we did. Only the children could prove that what we did was good and right, and that would take time. Meanwhile I walked around the block.

But you cannot, I found, discourage parents where their children are concerned. They are a stubborn lot, a persistently inquiring lot, and I am thankful that they are so. If they weren't, such a school as ours perhaps could not exist. For, finding we would not talk about it, they came to see with their own eyes and hear with their own ears. They watched their children and discerned the effects of the school on them.

That their findings were satisfactory, I can only assume from the result. How else could a Mere Father have made such a confession as this:

"My every domestic move has been dictated by your authority. The very location of the house I live in was determined by you. My availability as husband and father was conditioned by my willingness to adopt the ways of a C. and C. School family. Our domestic schedule is fixed by you—our daily and weekly comings and goings . . . The spiritual outlook of family life is colored by what your teachers think of our kids. A kind word for manners and morals, or even brains, sets up the household for a week—and vice versa . . ."

There was a neighbor of the school, consistently critical of what we were doing, who one day came in and surprised me by applying for admission for her three children. I asked her what had changed her mind about us.

"Your children have changed my mind," she answered. "They are the most interesting children I meet anywhere."

From the earliest days we knew that it was not possible to do good work with little children without the help of their parents. I might walk around the block to avoid them, but the doors of the school were always open to them, they were always welcome to sit in the classroom or stand in the yard, and the teachers, far from waiting for them to come, made it a point to seek them out for conferences.

It was a matter of policy for the teacher to arrange at least one conference early in the year with each parent, and to call the first group meeting of the year. Since we had no system of marks or report cards, these conferences kept parents informed of their children's progress. With the older groups the parents were invited to read the teacher's annual report.

While we made the school and the teachers always accessible to them, and invited them to spend as much time as they could spare, I believe they would have come anyway. If the development of their children under our methods was of interest to us, it was still more personally interesting to them. There have been mothers who spent very nearly as much time in the school as their children—and made themselves useful while doing so.

The effect the school has had on their homes I can report only by what they have told me. They have come to live in our neighborhood to be close to the school, have chosen apartments with an eye to play space as they have seen it used in the school (blocks do require plenty of space!), have closed their eyes to damage by water and fire and the spattering of paint and clay in the interests of child experimentation —or, more ingeniously, have arranged their homes so as to endure the experiments without the damage.

More than this, they have confessed to finding their children far more interesting than they thought children could be. This is most generally a paternal confidence. "A father hopes to have fun playing ball with his son, going fishing together if he is a fisherman, taking his son to the baseball game and the circus—but I'll be darned if I ever dreamed a Sunday walk down the street with my seven-year-old son would be an exciting experience!" Thus one father articulated his astonishment at the freshness and lively interest which familiar things took on when seen through his son's eyes.

This same father took his cue from his children, and invented a family institution, the "mystery trip." It was nothing more than a Sunday expedition for the family, and it might start in the quiet canyons of Wall Street, take in a ferry ride to Hoboken, and end in the Mediaeval armor collection of the Metropolitan Museum. Its essence was variety, surprise, ample opportunity for fresh air, and the flexibility to change pace and direction according to the family's mood —or energy. The inspiration for these trips, the very idea of spending his Sunday wandering around the city with his two young children, was a frank steal from the school. He had the humility to admit he had never spent his Sundays to such good advantage before.

There have always been parents who enjoyed their children—the school did not create them. What the school may have done, what such parents say the school has done, was to set their imaginations spinning around new experiences to share with their children, new fields to explore together. They have found themselves, say these parents, less and less dependent on organized entertainment, on the movies, for example, on theatrical performances especially presented for children and generally no treat to the adults (no treat to the children, either, in many cases). They have found their children, no less than themselves, ready with ideas for things to do.

But fathers have perpetually locked horns with the school on two subjects—and I suppose they always will. One is the circus, and the other is baseball. I have no objection to the circus in principle: the country circuses I remember from my own childhood were fine. But the circus today has grown into a monster of bigness which no child should be asked to confront. Three rings and two stages, with heaven knows what going on up under the roof of Madison Square Garden, with trapezes and tightropes and death-defying leaps—it is just too much. And when parents have had the effrontery besides to take their children out of school to subject them to such an experience as this, I have had no compunction in venting my wrath on them.

As for baseball, I have protested, but not with much success. There is something like a magic circle which encloses a father, his son, and a World Series game, and I have never quite got my foot into the circle. I have no objection to baseball, but every objection to children in crowds. But at this point the fathers have looked at me coldly, and I wash my hands of them.

I have been happy to see a new democracy growing between these parents and their children. With children who are accustomed to group discussion and to whom the will of the majority is more than just big words, a family conference quite obviously is a better way to reach a decision than any method which smacks of parental autocracy. Some parents slip naturally into this democratic system, reserving only the most serious matters—such as questions of health—for the flat *yes* or *no*. They have not had to pretend to take their children's judgment seriously, for in all honesty they have found much of it good and sound. Fathers as well as mothers have told me with frank delight that their children were "on to them"—like the mother who told me how, one evening, on the maid's day off, she had made her son put down his comic book and dry the dishes for her, and then, when he sulked, had angrily driven him from the kitchen because the manner of his doing the unwelcome task offended her by its ungraciousness. Later, ashamed of her own bad temper, she asked him what he thought about the incident.

"It all depends," he answered without rancor, "on whether you wanted the job done. If you really wanted the dishes dried, did it matter whether I smiled while I dried them? It would be nicer, I guess, but it couldn't be so important." Wisdom from an eleven-year-old, but wisdom nevertheless!

But since we are talking about parents, we must look at all kinds. For there are all kinds of parents, just as there are all kinds of children, just as there are all kinds of human beings. This new freedom for children is not easy for all parents, nor indeed for any parents all the time. The wails of dismay which have come to my ears through three decades have been many and various, mostly amusing but sometimes with dark overtones. I do not blame the parents for protesting. It is the same as putting a traditional teacher suddenly in charge of one of our free and noisy classrooms. A traditionally reared parent is quite as much at sea before a child who questions parental authority at every point. In our early years the conflict was sharper than it is today, and more visible. I am not sure but that open battle, as it was in those days, is not better than some of the concealed resentments and buried antagonisms I have found today. The pity of it is that it works both ways, to the child's disadvantage as well as the parent's. A free life at school and nineteenth-century discipline at home are a perplexing problem to any child.

To do all our parents justice, they have striven mightily, though with uneven success, to make the leap from their own traditional childhood to the freedom they have approved in principle for their children. They have tried to "reason things out," have worked the long way round to achieve a result for which traditional discipline had a ready short cut. They have worn thin both patience and ingenuity, and often enough have come to the school in despair.

"How can I get them to pick up after themselves?" I could only answer that they pick up most faithfully at school. But at school there is a time for picking up, and a practical reason for picking up—to make ready for the next thing the children want to do—and with the little ones there is a game of picking up in which, I have softly pointed out, the teacher and any other adults who happen to be around also join.

Picking up might be made a little easier. One mother hit upon the device of a junk box, into which odds and ends of all kinds could be thrown just to get them out of the way; even a young child is willing to hunt through such a squirrel's nest of oddments next time to find something he wants. It is really a new kind of game.

And maybe picking up is not so important. If a boy has a little space to himself where he can leave his model plane and his tools—and also the shavings of balsa wood on the floor; if a little girl can be given a corner where the damp concoction of breakfast cereal and lettuce and breadcrumbs she has fixed for her doll's supper can be left to "cook" overnight; if private little areas can be set apart where children's work— all right, mess, if you insist—can lie without disturbing the family, why should they pick up each time? They will pick up and clean up when they are ready for the next job.

But while the doll's mess is easily relegated to an inconspicuous corner, not so the child's own mess at the dinner table. Their children's table manners are a constant sore point with our parents. But, I have pointed out, the children eat only five meals a week in school compared with sixteen at home. Where was the responsibility for bad table manners, in the face of such statistics? All but the hardiest parent must blush and fall silent before this argument.

But the argument is specious. There is more to the question of table manners than merely school versus home. In the days of parental autocracy children were badgered into minding their manners. At whatever cost to their little individualities they were hounded into the forms of good behavior with adults every day of their lives. Today's child is not taught to curtsey or bow when he enters a room; he speaks when he has a mind to, and does not say *please* or *thank you* like a parrot, but because he knows the meaning of the words and their acceptability in social behavior.

If he eats like a little animal, spurning fork and napkin, this too is part of his more natural, unforced growth. When he wants to eat with his parents, and understands that forks and napkins are an essential requirement for that privilege, he will learn to use them.

I have pitied our parents, caught as they are between two worlds. They cannot use the old ways with their children, and are not trained in the new. Almost every step is a step into the dark, and their way is thorny and full of pitfalls. Persistently bad eating habits may be more than just animal freedom; they may be a weapon in a child's hand against an insensitive parent, or an unconscious bid for help in a child struggling with some deeper trouble. Parents who want to

save their children from emotional broken bones must learn
to watch for such distress signals.

Recently a parent told me a story which took me back almost twenty years. Her own children were as yet unborn, when she had as her guest the six-year-old son of an older friend, a boy who was one of our school youngsters. The child's parents deposited Peter with his hostess and went on to a dinner party elsewhere. At dinner, Peter, eating carefully and neatly, asked a pointed question.

"Do you know why Mommy and Daddy didn't stay here for dinner?"

"Yes, because they were expected at a dinner party. That's why they left you with me."

"Oh, no," said Peter, with positive glee. "That's not the reason at all. It's because Daddy has such terrible table manners that Mommy is ashamed to eat out with him at anyone's house!"

Peter's hostess, who knew what a slanderous attack this was on an impeccable gentleman, got to the truth of the matter with Peter's mother. Peter's father had been irked by the boy's eating habits, had nagged him about them, had finally sent him from the table in disgrace—and this was Peter's revenge! Yes, I pity the poor parent. He must weigh his every word!

But Peter's hostess suspected there was more to this than a mere dispute about table manners, and knowing the child and his family, I know she was right. His parents were both deep in absorbing careers, so deep that not only their children but their marriage itself eventually suffered.

I have seen many mothers too wrapped up in their own purposes, however worthy, to give their children any attention, and then all at once, in an access of guilt, make it up to them with some large and expensive demonstration of affection. There was one such mother who protested against our way of celebrating birthdays in the younger groups with a simple party—ice cream and cake and some happy games at the end of the school day. She scorned such a party, which was no party at all, with the children not even dressed up in party clothes, but wearing the grimy overalls in which they had played all day. We told her we disapproved of big parties for little children; the simple party in school which we prescribed was quite enough excitement for a five-year-old.

"How can I show my little girl I love her," she blurted finally, "unless I give her a beautiful big party for her birthday?" I wondered why a little girl must wait through a whole barren year for the one day on which her mother could show she loved her. But the party was duly given, over our objection, and the little girl spent the last hour of it huddled in her room behind a closed door, her hands over her ears to shut out the noise of twenty-five child guests, her party frock rumpled and stained with tears—an exhausted little victim of her mother's overwhelming sense of guilt. Children thrive better on love in smaller doses, more frequently administered.

Modern people, especially modern women, so many of whom have careers outside the home, have a profound dilemma to solve when they have children, and I offer no censure. I can only quote one working mother whose solution for herself and her children—to give up her work during their early years—so far has brought them all happiness: "They need us desperately while they need us—but for such a short time. Surely if we are going to have children we owe them those few years. If we have them, and then are stingy in giving ourselves, we're criminal—and if we don't have them at all, what we miss!"

Words, naughty words, are another sore point, perhaps even sorer than table manners. Parents have been driven nearly frantic by periodic epidemics of bathroom language which have swept through a group. There is nothing new in this problem; children and four-letter words have always had a natural affinity for each other. Let me set one bug-a-boo at rest right now: most psychologists are agreed that the manifestation has nothing whatever to do with sex. But even though it has no more sinister implications than appear on the surface, it is hard to endure. What is a parent to do in an era when washing the mouth out with soap is no longer an acceptable retort?

One mother and father agreed to teach their youngsters a lesson, and at dinner that night the two adults held the floor with a dialogue liberally spiced with all the offensive words their children liked so much and a few dredged up out of their own childhood—honest folk, they knew well that not only at City and Country School but in the traditional schools as well, children learn many things not on the curriculum!

The experiment worked almost too well: the children were aghast; one of them jumped up and ran out of the room in tears! That was the end of the pestilence in that family.

I followed this method myself once when a group of Twelves had a belated attack of bathroom talk. I went up to their classroom and shot their favorite words right back at them, mentioning that I had known all those words and many more for years, but I'd found more interesting conversation by the time I was twelve! It cleared the air of the Twelves' classroom like magic.

But this is a drastic treatment, more than most decently brought up adults can nerve themselves to. The best treatment for these outbreaks is to ignore them.

This too, I am in honor bound to point out, has some slight dangers. One dainty little five-year-old brought home a fine-sounding phrase, which she tried out on her mother in various combinations for a solid afternoon without getting so much as a raised eyebrow in response. Finally the child burst out in a fury of frustration, "Mommy, don't you know that's the worst thing you can say in the English language?"

Her mother agreed, but explained pleasantly that she had heard it long ago and didn't find it particularly interesting.

It took a year and a half, but this little girl got even, much as Peter of the messy eating habits had wreaked vengeance on his father. No untoward language had come from those youthful lips until one day, when she was six-and-a-half, she cornered a friend of her mother's and repeated the offensive phrase (pronouncing it quite accurately by this time). When the friend expressed mild surprise, this little innocent retorted airily, "Oh, I learned it from Mommy—she says it all the time!"

All this our parents must endure, and patiently. There is enough truth in those well worn jokes about progressive school children to make me wince now and then, for I know that the modern parent is a sacrifice, and not always a willing one, to the new bill of rights for children. I cannot blame him for wondering ruefully, on occasion, whether the result will prove the sacrifice worth while—he must wait nearly the rest of his life to learn the answer. But I do blame him for failing to understand some very important things about children.

I think parents have astonished me most by their failure to appreciate their children. The common belief that a parent is always swollen with pride, that Johnny's latest remark is Father's favorite topic of conversation, that a mother can see no wrong in her own offspring—in my experience all this has scarcely a grain of truth. I have had hard work through the years to sell parents on the charm, intelligence, wit, and general excellence of their children!

Perhaps it is true, as one mother pointed out, that parents rarely see children at their best. All the least pleasant things have to be got through at home—the endless routines of scrubbing behind the ears, of dressing and undressing, of mealtime and bedtime—and most clashes occur at the end of the day, when parents and children are both at a low ebb of friendliness and patience. In the reports of friends at whose homes a child has visited a mother often fails to recognize the youngster she is so familiar with. Why can't he behave like that at home?

The answer is embedded in the question—it is because he is at home. Because at home he is himself, relieved of the pressure of making himself socially acceptable; he could not maintain that level of excellent behavior indefinitely or he would burst, and where else but at home can he relax?

And if the pressure of good behavior is relieved at home,

we must remember that other, more subtle pressures are there in full force, sometimes destructive force. The emotional relationships with father and mother, with sisters and brothers, go deeper than any superficial social contact, and all too often they are not of the kind to bring out the best in a child. Who knows what makes a good child at school behave like a little demon at home—who but his parents? And if they don't know, I suggest it is up to them to find out. In this case a little child cannot lead them. He can only fly his frantic distress signals, voice his desperate, concealed cries for help.

Beyond their discontent with the effect of freedom on their children's social behavior, parents have gone along with us remarkably well in our educational policies, have indeed strengthened our hand with their enthusiasm and their eagerness to understand and to learn. Their very complaints, for the most part, have been made in the spirit of asking for help; they have come to the school as to a doctor, telling of discomfort at the dinner table and anguish at bedtime, and what can the doctor prescribe for the family's better social health?

But one point of our educational method with their children has been most consistently questioned. Why, they demand, must we wait to teach reading at seven, in the second grade? The traditional schools have always taught reading in the first grade. I have explained each time that neither six nor seven is the biological age for learning to read—frankly, I don't know what the biological age is, or if there is one; I myself learned to read, sitting in my grandmother's lap, somewhere between four and five, and plenty of normal children, no matter when they are exposed to reading, do not really learn until the age of eight or nine! The age of six has been established by nothing more scientific than simple custom. I once asked John Dewey why six was the accepted age for beginning reading; his answer was that nobody knew what else to do with children after five!

Why we teach reading at seven rather than six is explained earlier in these pages, in the chapter on seven-year-olds. But why parents so persistently ask us this question is another matter; the reasons some of them give are revealing, and not always flatteringly so.

Parents are anxious to have their children begin reading, they say, because reading is the beginning of their education —a curious hangover from traditional thinking about education, this identification of learning with books. My entire life, and our school, and this very book have been devoted to the cause of demonstrating that education does not begin with books, but with life; that books are only a part of a child's learning, not even the most important part. He will come to books in good time, but let him not lean on them too much, or too soon.

A frank and rather callous confession has been that once a child learns to read he is less trouble. He can be sent off to a corner with a book and that's the end of him for a while. I would not even dignify this complaint, so much more concerned with a parent's convenience than a child's best interest, by recording it here, but it has been too frequent to ignore.

The strangest reason of all for impatience is that a parent is waiting anxiously to see whether his child is mentally normal—and reading is the test. I have had people roar with laughter at this, but to me it is not funny. I could explain, and I have, that some quite low-grade intelligences have been known to conquer reading, and that even to a not very observant parent, an abnormal child is likely to give plenty of signs of deficiency before the age of six.

But parents, no less than children, are beset with fears, and the fear of abnormality is a common one. I sympathize, up to a point. Where I stop sympathizing and become impatient in my turn is when I see how shallow such a parent's concern may be, and how easily appeased. Once satisfied that the child has the requisite number of hands and feet and eyes and ears, that it has enough brain to learn to talk and to read, such a parent is content to leave the child thereafter to make his way through the stormy seas of growing up without further attention. It would never occur to him that his child may apparently learn to read at six or seven, and may turn out at nine or ten or even eleven to be suffering from a reading difficulty based on emotional disturbance, nearly as crippling as a low-grade intelligence.

Some quite remarkable work has been done with reading problems in recent years, and some of the experts in the field believe that reading difficulties—once physical causes such as poor eyesight have been eliminated—are an invariable sign of emotional disturbance. That they frequently are such a sign I do not doubt; I have seen reading difficulties coupled with plenty of other signs of emotional disturbance, perfectly apparent to any parent with eyes to see.

I have been angry with parents, not for visiting their own weaknesses on their children because too often, alas, they cannot help themselves—but for being slow to mark the distress signals, slow to see that their children are in trouble and need help. There are no bad children, only bad parents—that has become a cliché during my lifetime. When I began to learn about children it would have been a shocking statement to make. Yet, cliché or no, it is still painfully slow work to convince parents that a difficult child is an unhappy child, and they must seek the reason within themselves.

Parents of children who are in difficulties very often turn to a school like ours, and are disappointed when we cannot magically remove the problem. We have helped in many cases, but our school was designed for children of all kinds, not for special children—neither specially gifted children nor specially troubled children—and we have never been willing to keep a child whose difficulties made him too great a disturbance to the group. Parents have been cross with me when I have told them without mincing words that their child's problem is a home problem; yet most children's problems are home problems.

Childhood is a time of great happiness and great unhappiness—there is not much middle ground. Growing and learning are painful processes, painful for parent as well as child, but they have their radiant side too, and when there is some deep dislocation, some hidden unbalance which makes the unhappiness outweigh the happiness, it is time to do something about it.

So I have been of two minds about parents all my life, half the time wondering why they sometimes give so little of themselves to their children—and the other half of the time convinced that children would be better off without them altogether. It is at these latter times, no doubt, when I have been out of patience with their stubborn unwillingness to see a truth about children which is perfectly obvious to me, that I have heaped them with the insults they accuse me of.

But they are not entirely the browbeaten wretches they paint themselves, cowering before their children and their children's teachers. Once in a while they answer back—I remember one such time when a mother turned on us.

"Have you ever nursed a child with a temperature of a hundred and four?" she blazed. "I thought not! Well, until you have, don't think you know everything there is to know about children, either!"

I don't suppose we do. I don't suppose all of us who have worked with children, plus all the parents who have cared for them, know everything about children, or ever will. All we can do is try to penetrate the mystery, veil by veil, and piece out our meager knowledge with common sense and wholesome, nourishing love.